FLOW IN THE OFFICE

FLOW IN THE OFFICE

Implementing and Sustaining Lean Improvement

BY CARLOS VENEGAS

New York

Most Productivity Press books are available at quantity discounts when purchased in bulk. For more information, contact our Customer Service Department (888-319-5852). Address all other inquiries to:

Productivity Press
444 Park Avenue South, 7th Floor
New York, NY 10016
United States of America
Telephone: 212-686-5900
Fax: 212-686-5411
E-mail: info@productivitypress.com

ProductivityPress.com

Library of Congress Cataloging-in-Publication Data

Venegas, Carlos.
    Flow in the office : implementing and sustaining lean improvements / by Carlos Venegas.
        p. cm.
    Includes index.
    ISBN 978-1-56327-361-2 (alk. paper)
    1. Office management. 2. Organizational effectiveness. 3. Industrial efficiency. I. Title.
    HF5547.V43 2008
    651.3—dc22

                                                                    2007034845

    11 10 09 08 07 5 4 3 2 1

CONTENTS

ACKNOWLEDGMENTS

This work is more than the sum of my own thoughts and experiences. It reflects the support of a number of generous individuals who bring with them their imagination and spirit of collaboration. Many of these people enrich my life in any number of ways, not only in their assistance with this book. I am grateful for their friendship and willingness to share.

I received insights on writing this book from Al Lopus, Sherry Thompson, Doug Taylor, Doric Olson, Terry Leers, and Shayne Fillmore.

My friends and colleagues, Bob Martin and Vance Butler, went out of their way to share their insights, which were many and greatly appreciated.

I would like to thank consultant Ann Dorgan for her contributions on sustaining a continuous improvement culture. She stimulated my thinking with her ideas, energetic spirit, and passion for research.

I would like to thank Lismary deLemos for her assistance in redefining waste in an office environment and for her ability to mirror my thoughts in a way that helped me see and articulate them more clearly.

My author friend, Ben Sherman, helped me stay productive in the writing process by sharing many of his writing tricks.

In this book, I placed emphasis on the concept of clarity, with the valuable aid of Mary Beth O'Neill and Roger Taylor, both colleagues and teachers.

Finally, I would like to thank my wife and colleague, Marilyn Venegas, for her unflagging support in this project.

INTRODUCTION

The idea for this book took shape at a lean conference presentation I delivered on implementing lean in a nonfactory work environment. In my presentation, I recounted a project where my clients wanted to improve a customer order process. What made the project compelling was the challenge: how to involve nontechnical employees in developing a process improvement solution that would almost certainly be technical.

The team members did a fabulous job (their results are detailed in Chapter 1). Their performance was beyond that which they thought they were capable and certainly beyond what the management expected. Interestingly, their capability was there all along, dormant and untapped. What made the difference to the team's performance was the "space for potential" created by our unique *kaizen*[1] workshop format, assembled from lean standard tools, project management tools, and organizational development principles.

The content of my presentation was sufficiently intriguing that a publisher invited me to expand it into book form. This book is an examination of the principles, techniques, and tools I used to conduct that kaizen, and a tool kit for readers to apply and create their own kaizen at their workplace.

LEAN IS SIMPLE AND ELEGANT

I became involved in lean business because I loved its simplicity and elegance. Eventually, the efficiencies that lean affords became my secondary objective. The positive impact that lean can have on people became my prime motivator, and what captured my attention. That impact has given me the energy and determination to carry the lean banner through thick and thin. For example, once during a kaizen event, a woman jogged past me, obviously on an errand for her lean kaizen team. As she passed me, she exclaimed with a wide grin and a laugh, "I'm having fun!"

Implementing lean can be hard, but it has been among the most enjoyable endeavors I've had in my business career. Why? It is because lean liberates hidden talents and capacities in everyone involved, even as it unleashes value.

Although implementing lean can be hard, process improvement itself is easy, at least once you know the principles of lean. In fact, for the initiated, lean principles often seem like solid common sense. Most of it *is* common sense. The *hard* part is people.

Without the active engagement of employees—and management—lean goes nowhere. Without people, lean is relegated to a collection of interesting ideas that fills the pages of books and documents, which, in turn, adorn bookshelves. It is people who bring life to lean, and paradoxically, lean can create a productive space in which people can blossom, bringing into full expression their talents and capacities.

LEAN MOVES FROM THE SHOP FLOOR TO THE OFFICE

For many years, lean has worked on the shop floor. As I saw at the conference that inspired this book, people now want to know how it can be used in the office—how to translate and transition lean manufacturing principles into the lean office. Therefore, this is a practical book about how I apply lean principles and tools in an office environment. It is not the only way, or in every case, the best way. It's simply a way that works for me, and has worked for the many teams I have coached to successful outcomes.

WHY LEAN FLOWS

Lean is a term popularized by James Womack and Daniel T. Jones in their book *Lean Thinking: Banish Waste and Create Wealth in Your Corporation.*[2] Lean refers to the Toyota Production System (TPS), which was pioneered by Taiichi Ohno at the Toyota Motor Company. Womack and Jones describe lean as an approach to "manage customer relations, the supply chain, product development, and production operations."[3]

Ohno says that the "basis of the Toyota Production System is the absolute elimination of waste."[4] To work toward this goal, the TPS rests on two fundamental principles:

1. Just-in-time (JIT) production

2. Autonomation (also known as *jidoka,* that is, automation with human intelligence)

In a *just-in-time* production environment, material, data, and information flow to a workstation in only the amounts needed for a particular operation at a particular time. This allows the system to minimize the amount of "work-in-process," or WIP. Reducing WIP allows for right-sized workstations and can actually increase the velocity and flexibility of a product's flow through the system.

Jidoka highlights the need to embed quality in the manufacturing process. If any defective process or object is discovered during the manufacturing process, the activity stops automatically, allowing the concerned people to correct the defect. Jidoka fosters high-quality parts and processes, which are a prerequisite for successful JIT.

Whereas the concept of "automation" focuses on reducing labor, autonomation (jidoka) focuses on improving quality. This frees people to focus on other value-added work.

Lean has been viewed by many as a product of the factory environment. Over the last 40 years, it has been refined and proven to be among the most effective strategies to improve operational productivity. An *Economist*[5] article gives lean the credit for uncommonly rapid productivity growth in the U.S. manufacturing sector between 2001 and 2006.

Clearly, lean works in a factory environment—but that is not why you are reading this book. You want to know how lean works in the office or nonfactory environment. To understand how lean can work in the office environment, you need to understand the underlying principles. When you apply the underlying principles to office processes, you can enjoy the same kind of improvements that others have experienced in the factory or on the shop floor.

LEAN IS AN OPERATIONAL STRATEGY

Harvard Business School professor, and one of the best-known authorities on competitive strategy, Michael Porter, draws a distinction between business strategy and what I call *operational* strategy:[6]

- Business strategy, according to Porter, is about making choices and about deliberately choosing to be different. You need to offer a value proposition, different from your competitors', to your customers.

- In contrast, operational strategy does not focus on making choices. It focuses on maintaining and improving the health and effectiveness of the organization, and the company as a whole.

Lean is an operational strategy, not a business strategy. It offers a superb way to eliminate waste, reduce cost, improve customer satisfaction, reduce cycle times, and improve other performance metrics. Lean does not tell you, however, the direction in which to take your business. Instead, it helps you become more competitive by enhancing your efficiency, productivity, and quality. I tell my clients to use lean in service to their business strategy.

SCALING SUCCESS WITH LEAN

Lean is the attempt of the rest of the business world to understand and harness that which Toyota has so gloriously done—rise above crushing obstacles. To us as individuals and as members of organizations, the rise of Toyota is mythic: an entity crushed during World War II, emerging from the rubble with the building blocks of what would become a manufacturing powerhouse—among the most admired in the world.

In our own evolutions, we bring our unique history and context. These are not the same as Toyota's in 1947, or typical of today's practices for that matter. For this reason, I share with you principles for you to apply (not to plug-and-play) as appropriate to your unique circumstances. Every situation is unique, and while most of the principles in this book may be universal, their application is not. Can we learn from others and adopt best practices? Yes, of course, but the point is to consider your unique situation when applying the principles.

HOW THIS BOOK IS STRUCTURED

This book has been structured along the lines of a typical lean implementation (see Figure I-1).

Step	Action	Chapter
1	Establish the business case for lean	1
2	Learn about lean in the office environment	2 and 3
3	Map the value stream	4
4	Prepare for and conduct an office kaizen	5 and 6
5	Sustain the gains	7

Figure I-1. Implementing lean in the office

The book begins with establishing the business case for lean. **Chapter 1** features an overview of what others have experienced with lean in their businesses.

Learning about lean in the office environment follows next. **Chapters 2 and 3** examine the nature of flow in the office environment, how waste impedes that flow, and some of the lean concepts that are used to combat waste.

In **Chapter 4**, we look at a type of process mapping called "value-stream mapping." The value-stream map (VSM) process visualizes the current and improved process; then identifies, prioritizes, and schedules the improvement activities.

Preparation for an office kaizen and its implementation are covered in detail in **Chapters 5 and 6**.

Chapter 7, the final and perhaps, the most important chapter, deals with sustaining the kaizen improvements.

LEAN—LOOKING FOR THE GOOD

I work under the assumption that if you are in business, you must be doing something right. This holds true, even if you believe your organization to be in a dismal state of affairs, because the good stuff is really buried under well-intentioned but wasteful practices. As you begin to peel off and discard the wasteful practices, the more productive and powerful practices come into plain view—much like a camera coming into focus. You will not only discover what is right with what you currently do, but will also learn how to make your current practices even better.

With lean, you learn by doing. Sure, reading helps, discussion helps—but the real learning is in the action. As you learn, you will make mistakes, and you must be willing to face failure with the openness and curiosity of a confident scientist.

Exploring this new way may not be easy, but it is exciting. Whether you are interested in a specific topic, say kaizen, or have committed yourself to launching lean in your workplace, I hope you will discover useful nuggets in this book that combine your current thinking with the limitless possibilities of what lean can do for your business.

I wish you the best of success.

NOTES

1. The Japanese word kaizen means continuous improvement. Kaizen origi-
nated in Japan after World War II as an approach to improving productivity.
The objectives of kaizen include elimination of waste (elements that add cost
but not value), just-in-time delivery, and work standardization. In this book, I
also use kaizen to refer to a rapid-improvement workshop.

2. James Womack and Daniel T. Jones, *Lean Thinking: Banish Waste and
Create Wealth in your Corporation* (New York: Simon & Schuster, 1996).

3. Womack, 9.

4. Taiichi Ohno, *Toyota Production System: Beyond Large-Scale Production*
(New York: Productivity Press, 1988), 4.

5. http://www.economist.com/business/PrinterFriendly.cfm?story_id=7119428

6. http://www.fastcompany.com/magazine/44/porter.html

CHAPTER 1

THE CASE FOR LEAN IN THE OFFICE

Computers are found everywhere in nonfactory environments, but they are only as effective as the processes set to facilitate their use. This book documents a method to improve processes, whether they involve computers or not, in office environments. One particular case study involves a team that worked to improve its order/production scheduling and billing process. Using the process described in this book, the team achieved the following positive results:

- It reduced scheduling cycle time by 58%.

- It increased scheduling productivity by 25%.

- It reduced schedulers' travel distance by 86%.

Figure 1-1 illustrates this team's success.

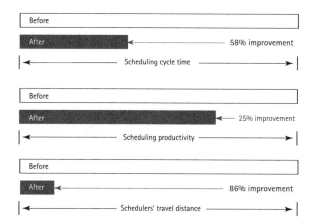

Figure 1-1. Team improvements using the process described in this book

This team faced an interesting project for a number of reasons. First, it was the first nonfactory kaizen it had undertaken. The group was familiar with lean and had completed several successful shop-floor kaizens, but some wondered how the team would be able to apply lean principles to office work.

Second, parts of the production scheduling and billing process were computerized. Although this delivers certain efficiencies, computing can pose challenges for two reasons: the processes are "invisible" when they occur in the system, and the team evaluating the existing processes and designing solutions was largely nontechnical. Would they be able to make the invisible processes visible in order to act on them? Did this largely nontechnical team have the right skills to devise efficient solutions? With the help of this new lean kaizen process, the answer to these questions was *yes*.

These results may seem impressive, and they are; yet these impressive results are typical of lean teams. In this author's experience, with scores of process improvement projects, teams achieved improvements that ranged from 15% to 93%, although most improvements fall somewhere in the mid-range.

The creation of customer value with minimal waste using Lean has a guaranteed place in front-line services as much as it does in manufacturing-line processes. The use of Lean has a clear impact on the product or service. Even in manufacturing environments, office processes can account for as much as 80% of the lead time.[1] Inefficiencies within office or service environments (i.e., waste) claim as much as 80% of an employee's timecard or even more, depending on the industry.

What if office processes are not the company's main business? Does it make sense to focus on nonproduction processes? The answer is a resounding *Yes!*

Nonproduction workers have a significant impact on productivity. In some cases, nonproduction workers, including "managerial, technical, and support staff,"[2] can have a greater impact on overall productivity than production workers. In many circumstances, "the productivity of nonproduction workers...becomes critical to improving factory productivity."[3]

LEAN WORKS IN A BROAD RANGE OF SERVICE INDUSTRIES AND MANY TYPES OF OFFICE WORK

There are numerous examples of Lean in service (i.e., nonmanufacturing) industries. For instance, the application of lean principles in various areas of the healthcare sector has seen results that reduce annual increases in FTEs (full-time employees) despite a no-layoff policy. Lean principles help the staff and patients eliminate waste through continuous improvement (including redesign) of processes. This not only results in better quality, but also in less rework and fewer staff members. In the long run, this reduces the need to replace employees as they retire or leave.

For example, a group of regional hospitals and insurance companies use lean principles to improve service standards. These groups recorded up to 85%

reduction in infections contracted at hospitals (as shown in Figure 1-2) and managed to cut costs from deaths due to coronary bypass problems by around $1.7 million.[4] Similarly, a group of vision care hospitals in India redesigned their work flow and patient flow to provide high-precision cataract surgeries at low costs.[5]

Figure 1-2. Lean in health care

Information technology is another cutting-edge sector that has benefited from lean. *Lean software development* is all about reducing project time by eliminating waste and delivering nearly zero defects (which further reduces cycle time).

Likewise, there are countless reasons to improve nonfactory processes: improve quality, reduce cost, and shorten lead times are three common ones. Lean transforms waste into available capacity (e.g., time released due to reduced cycle time). Financial benefits accrue as sound decisions are made on the use of that newly available capacity. Whatever the reason, lean offers tools, methods, and principles to revolutionize the way work is done.

Customer service is a front-line function; one that can build strong relationships with the customer when well executed, or poison any well-intentioned marketing program when it flounders and stumbles. A *Business Week* article reports on the use of lean methods in the customer-service operation of a home builder[6] that, by reducing variation and complexity, provided customers with simplified decision making while saving the company between 5% and 10%.

Behind customer services lies the back office. Back-office services, too, have benefited from lean methods, and some initiatives show impressive numbers (as shown in Figure 1-3). One back-office service provider redesigned its operations using the Toyota Production System. Their "Toyota-like efficiency" had the following results:

- A 43% improvement in productivity

- Rework reduction from 18% to 2%, representing an 88% improvement

- A reduction of import approvals from 30 days to 15 days[7]

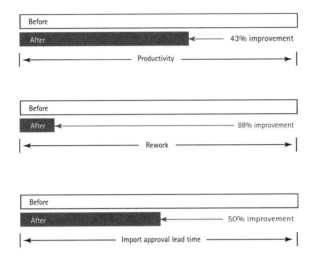

Figure 1-3. Back office improvements

Even the public sector has embraced lean. The Iowa state government has reported dramatic reductions in several permitting process lead times; for example, as shown in Figure 1-4:

- Wastewater permitting lead time was reduced from 425 days to 15 days.

- Landfill permitting was shortened from 187 days to 30 days.

- Amazingly, corrective-action decisions over defective underground storage tanks once took 1,124 days; after lean improvements, the lead time is 90 days.

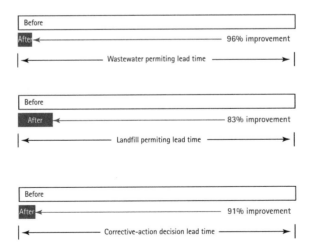

Figure 1-4. Lean in the public sector

These are impressive results indeed. Almost anyone can enjoy those results. The first step is to understand the concept of "value."

HOW LEAN DEFINES *VALUE* AND *VALUE ADDED*

Womack and Jones define *value* as "a capability provided to a customer at the right time at an appropriate price, as defined in each case by the customer."[8] The lean definition of value is customer driven, and that is a key distinction.

Value is defined from the perspective of the customer; be it an end customer or an intermediate one. This value must be identified and explicitly stated in terms of how the product or service meets the customer's requirements at the right time, at the right price, in the right amount, at the right quality, and done right the first time. The fundamental step to identifying customer-defined value is to develop an understanding of why the customer is buying the company's product or service. How the customer values the product can give insights into what is relevant to the customer and what is not.

It is deceptively easy to fall into the trap of defining value from the perspective of the firm rather than from the point-of-view of its customer. For example, an office worker, Tom, spends extra time and money to print a report on blue paper (because he thinks the person receiving the report will appreciate that it looks different from all other memos in her in bin), whereas the customer (in this case, a fellow office worker named Sally) would rather have the information in an e-mail because Sally values the *information*, not the paper on which it is printed, and because she transfers the information into a spreadsheet for analysis anyway. So she really doesn't need a printed report, regardless of what color paper it's printed on. Tom considers the activity of printing on blue paper as creating value for Sally; however, the blue paper printout is irrelevant to Sally because her interest lies solely in the *data*.

Once value is understood as being customer defined, another question arises: Does the process add value to the "thing" going through the process? In other words, can the process, or the steps within the process, be described as *value added*, that is, changing the thing in a way that the customer values. An activity or action is value added if the customer perceives it as adding significant value to the output, benefiting him or her substantially, and is willing to pay for the improvements.

For an action to be value added, it must meet all three of the following criteria:

1. The customer is willing to pay for the activity.

2. It must be done right the first time.

3. The action must modify the product or service at some level(s).

An activity or action that adds *cost* but no real value to a product or service is termed a *non-value-added* activity—which is *waste*.

To expand on the previous example, Tom's efforts in buying, stocking, and printing on blue paper were non-value-added to Sally. She would have to take that blue sheet of paper and rekey the information into a spreadsheet. Not only did Tom's efforts not add value to Sally, it also raised Tom's costs in terms of purchase of the blue paper, stocking it, and printing on it.

So what would be a value-added process in this case? Because the customer would rather have the information in an e-mail so she can cut and paste the data into her spreadsheet, sending an e-mail would be better. But why stop there? Here are other alternatives to consider:

- Could Tom simply send the data to her in a spreadsheet? Would that make it easier?

- What if Tom put the information directly into the spreadsheet for her?

- What if Sally could get the information from Tom's database herself, freeing Tom up to do something else, and allowing Sally to get the information when she was ready to use it?

Is any of this possible? Well, perhaps. One thing is for certain: Tom and Sally are the best people to answer that question. They need to talk to each other about it.

This book provides a structure for Tom and Sally (or in larger, more complex organizations, all the Toms and Sallys) to understand and analyze the situation, develop and test solutions and improvements, and then implement those solutions and improvements.

In the quest to isolate "value-added" activities, it is vital to recognize its converse—waste. Lean not only focuses on adding value, but also weeds out anything that blocks the flow of value to the customer. Chapter 2 looks at how to find possible sources of waste in your office.

NOTES

1. Anonymous, "The New Improvement Frontier," Strategic Direction, 21 (2005): 33-35.

2. John G. Wacker, Chen-Lung Yang, and Chwen Sheu, "Productivity of production labor, non-production labor, and capital: An international study," International Journal of Production Economics, 103 (2006): 864.

3. Ibid., 868-869.

4. Jon Miller, "Good News! Hospitals are Healing Themselves through Kaizen," May 16, 2006, www.gembapantarei.com

5. Jon Miller, "Streamlining Eye Surgery-Innovation in India," November 2, 2004, www.gembapantarei.com

6. Kathleen Kerwin, "A New Blueprint at Pulte Homes: CEO Dugas' Plan for Insulating the Red-hot Homebuilder from Downturns," Business Week, published October 3, 2005, downloaded from http://www.businessweek.com on September 25, 2006.

7. Steve Hamm, "Taking a Page from Toyota's Playbook: Wipro and Other Indian Info-Tech Companies are Boosting Efficiency by Emulating the Japanese Carmaker," Business Week, published August 22, 2005, downloaded from http://www.businessweek.com on September 25, 2006.

8. Womack and Jones, p. 311.

CHAPTER 2

FINDING WASTE IN THE OFFICE— SO YOU CAN ELIMINATE IT

Eradicating waste and maximizing value is central to the lean approach. Waste is anything that does not add value to a product or service. Simply put, it is anything for which the customer would not be willing to pay. Some forms of waste appear obvious; others may be latent or intangible. Eliminating waste allows value to flow with higher speed and quality through the business process.

Waste on the factory floor is relatively easy to spot. For example, it would be hard to miss a big pile of car parts waiting for a purchase order before moving toward assembly or an operator dozing away while waiting for the machine to complete its course. However, identifying waste in the service sector or in office processes is often more subtle and complex. Defects in a product appear more obvious than flaws in an intangible work method.

In office and administrative scenarios, the concepts of *value* and *waste* are implicit or hidden in intangible "products" and processes. Paradoxically, office waste and its consequences can be costlier than manufacturing wastes. An erroneous quote or a flawed design document can ruin businesses and cost millions. On the brighter side, the lean principles used to eliminate waste in a manufacturing setup can be applied to track and remove waste, and facilitate the flow of value in the office as well.

WHAT EXACTLY IS WASTE?

A metaphor popular among those familiar with the Toyota Production System is that of "the stream." The stream, which indicates flow, is the process that needs to be completed. Obstructions such as rocks or circuitous bends in the stream indicate waste—the factors that hamper or slow down the process. As you remove the rocks one by one, and straighten the course of the stream, the water begins to flow without stopping or slowing down. Waste can either *add friction* or *completely block the flow of value*. Friction weakens the interaction among the different elements of a typical office and impedes the flow of value. As a result, quality deteriorates, requiring more time and effort to achieve the desired results.

Every business entity aims to stay competitive by focusing on value-adding processes. However, consider these statistics:

- Administrative costs may consume 60% to 80% of the total cost of goods and services sold.[1]

- The proportion of non-value-adding activities in a typical manufacturing firm can range from 70%[2] to 95%![3]

- In a typical office scenario, the figures are not much different—non-value-added office and service work can range up to 95%.[4]

Ironically, the organization is often aware of only a very small percentage of this waste. This should give you some indication of the urgency to improve the efficiency of business processes.

FOUR TYPES OF WASTE

The office may be compartmentalized into four elements—information, process, physical environment, and people. Each of these elements could host a range of wastes, both obvious and dormant. This chapter identifies and classifies some of them. Before examining them in detail, however, a few clarifications are needed.

First, this list is by no means exhaustive. New and different elements of waste occur in individual offices. The ability to see the invisible and to unravel this hidden waste is the essence of successful lean implementation.

Second, some types of waste could appear in more than one lean office element. These may be reorganized in a way that best suits the specific context. Lean, practiced over time, can go beyond improvements in individual areas; it can increase overall productivity by making the entire process flow.

Third, some of the wastes on the list may seem similar—even identical. Many distinctions are included to help you recognize waste in your organization. Ignore a distinction that seems confusing or does not apply to you.

The measures identified to counter waste are generic suggestions. Every situation has unique properties, and so each countermeasure should be tailored to the situation. Some specific lean tools for eliminating waste are discussed in greater detail in Chapter 3.

The rest of this chapter takes a closer look at the four most common types of waste:

1. Information waste

2. Process waste

3. Waste in the physical environment

4. People waste (i.e., inefficiencies in how people work)

Information Waste

Information is to office and management functions what raw material is to manufacturing. In fact, the emergence of the knowledge economy has erased even this distinction. Today, information forms the basis for every decision, process, or action in any organization looking for competitive advantage. Consequently, information waste, in some form, leads to erosion or obstructions in the flow of value. Figure 2-1 offers a quick overview of twelve general types of information waste, and the next sections describe each type in more detail, with suggestions for how to prevent or eliminate such waste.

---

1. Redundant input and output of data
2. Incompatible information systems
3. Manual checking of data that has been entered electronically
4. Data dead-ends (i.e., data that is input but never used)
5. Reentering data
6. Converting formats
7. Unnecessary data
8. Unavailable, unknown, or missing data
9. Unclear or incorrect data
10. Data safety issues (i.e., lost or incorrect data)
11. Unclear or incorrect data definitions
12. Data discrepancies

Figure 2-1. Types of information waste

Redundant Inputs and Outputs

This type of information waste occurs when identical data inputs or outputs occur more than once without adding any extra value. In other words, the redundancy is built into the process.

Any redundancy takes up time, effort, and resources that would be better spent on adding value. For example, in healthcare offices, it is fairly common for patients to fill out multiple forms that ask the same or similar questions, and then patients are asked the same questions again by the medical assistant and the medical care provider. Admittedly, some repetition for verification is justified—after all, lives can be at stake—but working off a single source of information would enhance consistency and accuracy. Similarly, if members of a research team are not given clearly delineated job descriptions or tasks, they may end up wasting time looking for, and finding, the same data.

Suggestions for eliminating this type of waste:

— Check for redundancies and repetitions in processes, job descriptions, documents, data, and so on.

— Check across processes and functions; do not assume that redundancy can occur only within a particular process or function. For instance, the sales department may be hiring sales trainees "informally" when there is already a fully operational recruitment system in the HR portfolio.

— Make sure a task is performed only once (unless repetition is necessary), and by those who are best qualified to do it.

Incompatible Systems

This type of waste occurs when two or more systems are used in the same process, but they are unable to share data.

Incompatible systems provide numerous opportunities for mistakes to occur, and some of them can prove disastrous, as illustrated in the examples in the next sections. Multiple and incompatible systems also consume valuable computing and people resources. Incompatibility of data storage and retrieval systems is the primary culprit, in many cases, of insufficient or missing data.

For example, picture this all-too-familiar situation: A customer waits for an unreasonably long time while two or more staff members try to get relevant information out of two incompatible systems. Not only do the staff members look ridiculously inefficient, they are also seriously stressed out.

Another typical situation: A firm has one database system that stores the client's personal data, while another tracks his or her purchases of the firm's products or services. A salesperson would be empowered to deliver far greater value to the customer if the two systems could "talk" to each other or better still, if they could be merged into a single comprehensive database.

Another example: In the scheduling and billing process, three systems were used to track projects in the shop; one was a manual paper system, which fed into another computerized system that generated processed data, which in turn was printed out. Some of the data from that printout was keyed in, yet again, into a third system. Not only did this incompatibility sacrifice time, but it also introduced vulnerability to input errors.

Suggestions for eliminating this type of waste:

— Simplify processes and minimize the number of systems wherever possible.

— Simplify and clarify read-out and input fields in both physical and electronic forms; this helps reduce the likelihood of errors.

— Document your information systems clearly.

— When a process involves cross-functional or cross-level interaction, make the relevant data and documents available to all relevant employees.

— Involve all functions concerned when planning for new information or data storage systems.

— Communicate all decisions to the employees (again, across levels and functions) impacted by a new system at the earliest possible time—make the best use of simple communication tools like an Intranet or even notice boards.

Manual Checking

This type of waste occurs when electronic or electronically generated information is manually checked for accuracy, completeness, and so on.

For example, this occurs when an accountant manually performs the calculations already completed electronically, or when an executive secretary personally contacts employees to crosscheck information entered in the employee database. Both of these could be considered cases of effort redundancy, or manual checking. Manual verification defeats the purpose of automation and paperless offices.

Suggestions for eliminating this type of waste:

— Recognize that checking for mistakes indicates a failure in the system. Look for that failure, and fix it so you do not have to spend time rechecking.

— Keep in mind that this does not mean that you *compromise* on quality; on the contrary, this means that you *emphasize* quality at the start. The idea is to create processes that do not allow errors to enter the value stream.

Data Dead-Ends

This type of waste occurs when data flows through a system and then stops, not serving any purpose. This does not include archiving—although you need to be clear about why you are archiving and what should be archived; instead, this waste occurs when data is not used or never will be used.

Data dead-ends are different from unnecessary data. Dead-end data is information that is entered into or processed by a system and then not used.

For example, the author of this book analyzed a business-metric collection and reporting process with one of his clients. They mapped out her process in detail, showing every user interface and data entry, then tracked the data flow from screen to screen. It was discovered—to the client's surprise—that she was asking for more data than she actually used. That gave her an opportunity to make an informed choice: either use the data being provided, or stop requiring her people to report that particular data to her.

Data dead-ends are often a result of changes in the process *downstream* that have not been reflected or communicated *upstream*. The client with the scheduling and billing process just mentioned entered some product data into the system that dead-ended about a third of the way through the process. Perhaps 10 years earlier, the data held a purpose, but no one on the team could remember why they needed it in the first place. In this case, they removed that data field from the input screen.

Another example involves feeding metrics data into a database that generates business reports. Here are wasteful scenarios that commonly occur in these cases:

• The actual generated report doesn't use that data anymore.

• The user of the report either ignores the data or cannot act on the data.

• The report is not even used anymore.

This is a common phenomenon. How to find these data dead-ends is explained in Chapter 6.

Suggestions for eliminating this type of waste:

— Reflect on why the dead-end has occurred:

 • Is the information being provided even though it is not needed? If so, stop providing it.

 • Is a downstream process, which needs the data, not receiving it? If so, is the data really not needed, or is the downstream process getting the information in some other way? What's the best way for that downstream process to receive that information?

— The first step toward answering these questions is to begin at the end of the process and work backward toward the beginning of the process:

 • Which individual or team collected or provided it, and with what objective?

 • Is there a downstream need for the data that dead-ended? If so, figure out how to get the data to where it is supposed to go. If the data is not needed, then perhaps you should stop providing it.

Answers to these questions will help unblock the flow of information through the value chain.

Reentering Data

This type of waste occurs when the original input is flawed or lost, so it needs to be reentered.

The need to collect or enter data again occurs when information is either lost, incomplete, insufficient, or incorrect. Reentering data is undoubtedly a waste. This is distinct from redundant inputs and outputs; this is an unplanned event. Reentering data is frustrating to everyone involved and can result in delays or even lost deals. Remember Sally from Chapter 1? She was given a report in hard copy by Tom, an office worker, who went through extra time and cost to print that report on blue paper. Sally, who was Tom's customer, preferred that information in an e-mail so that she was spared the effort of feeding the same data onto a spreadsheet. Transferring the data from Tom's blue paper to a spreadsheet is a classic case of this type of waste.

Suggestions for eliminating this type of waste:

— Update data records and have systems in place for tracking usage.

— More important, analyze the use to which the data are put—it might give you insight into how it can be better presented and save the user time and effort.

— Verify information at the point of entry—incorporate this in the job description of staff responsible for data entry.

Converting Formats

This type of waste occurs when someone changes information from one format to another.

An example of this is taking information from a presentation and converting it into a report for a different audience. Sometimes this makes sense; you may, indeed, have to customize the presentation for different audiences. Often, however, it happens simply because of lack of standardized formatting.

Suggestions for eliminating this type of waste:

— Develop standards.

— Apply common formatting standards wherever possible, and communicate these standards to employees and customers.

— Before beginning to compile and present data, get all those who will use the information to decide on the format best suited to their needs.

— If multiple formatting is unavoidable, keep in mind that it may be more efficient to generate the multiple formats at the point of compilation.

Unnecessary Data

This type of waste occurs when you have data that is not used in any process. It may be left over from a previous process, or it may be "just-in-case" data.

For example, suppose a new trainee designer in an apparel-manufacturing firm is given a job description that includes "gain a thorough understanding of the apparel industry and the business environment." Among other things, the trainee comes up with a fifty-page report on the trends in cotton production over the last few decades. Although this may be an exaggerated situation, surveys confirm that a large number of reports and research documents in many organizations end up gathering dust. Unnecessary data is obviously a waste of time and effort, but it can also lead to confusion and complicate the process of finding relevant information.

Suggestions for eliminating this type of waste:

— Avoid gathering data that does not have any apparent relevance—either immediate or long term.

— In cases where information was previously gathered for a specific purpose, check with stakeholders about whether it is needed any more:

  • If that information is still needed, file it in a folder indicating the specific purpose for which the data can be used.

  • If that information is still *not* needed, get rid of it.

— Be as specific as possible when asking for facts, figures, or any other information.

— Spend more time up front understanding the users' data requirements.

Unavailable, Unknown, or Missing Data

This type of waste involves data that should be available to a particular person, group, or system, but isn't.

Everyone knows that crucial information is, or should be, somewhere in the system. Nevertheless, it cannot be traced. The hunt for data, often involving cross-functional communication, not only results in waste, but also leads to conflicts and a never-ending blame game. The causes of unavailable, unknown, or missing data are numerous. These are also addressed under other categories of waste.

Suggestions for eliminating this type of waste:

— Standardize your documents; this is another area that can benefit from standardization.

— Make the documentation and data storage systems easily accessible to all.

— Wherever applicable, ensure that file names and labels reflect the kind of data each file contains, as well as the departments or processes that are most likely to use the data.

Incorrect Data

Waste caused by incorrect data needs no further definition; this problem obviously causes waste in an office (or any environment).

For example, imagine the consequences of a sales forecast or market research document with a single wrong statistic. Surprisingly, data errors often go unspotted and can escalate into major catastrophes. In the information age, knowledge is power indeed. Accuracy in data is a prerequisite for any business process, and in certain areas like health care and pharmaceuticals, it can even mark the difference between life and death.

Here's another example: Several years ago, the author's healthcare provider contacted him regarding his step-daughter, Erica. They were calling concerning her healthcare issues. After a short while and some confusion, it became apparent that they had the wrong Erica. There was another patient in their system with the same name. The confusion was resolved without much inconvenience, but it could have been much worse. It turned out that the other Erica had diabetes. Should that mistake in identifying the right Erica happen while care is being administered, unhealthy results could have ensued.

To their credit, this healthcare provider has chosen to implement lean. Their service and customer satisfaction has improved. For example, 2 years ago, a particular procedure this author needed took *8 months to complete.* This includes the time from the patient making the first call for the first appointment, to when the patient actually received treatment. Today, the lead time for the same outcome has been *reduced to 1 month.*

Suggestions for eliminating this type of waste:

— Recognize that the source of the incorrect data may not be the source of the problem. More often than not, incorrect data indicates flaws or inefficiencies deeply embedded in some aspect of the process.

— Trace the true origin of the inaccuracies to help eliminate such errors in the future.

— Reduce the number of manual data inputs and data hand-offs. Each data input or hand-off is an opportunity for an error to occur.

— Simplify input and read-out forms and screens.

— Another way of preventing data errors is to ensure that the persons who require a particular piece of information are involved in briefing those responsible for collecting the information.

Data Safety Issues

Data safety is concerned with data loss or corruption.

In recent years, risk management and business continuity have become the focus of most organizations. The emphasis has now shifted to information security. The proliferation of the Internet and Intranets, and the transformation of data into paperless form have added new dimensions to data security.

For example, valuable customer information that has been gathered over the years and then left on a system, without adequate backup and storage, is not only exposed to data theft but also runs the risk of being wiped out in the event of a hardware problem. Any information left exposed could meet with the same fate. There have been numerous reports of companies losing laptops that contain sensitive information about their clients or employees. Policies need to be established that protect data from loss, theft, or misuse.

Suggestions for eliminating this type of waste:

— Back up data in more than one location.

— Use encryption for sensitive data.

— Establish version control—a way to keep track of how data files evolve—or other kinds of controls to ensure data integrity.

— Scrutinize the end-to-end movement of data to help identify and plug loopholes.

— Implement an operational backup and recovery plan.

Unclear or Incorrect Data Definitions

This type of waste occurs when descriptions of data in database tables are unclear or incorrect.

For example, suppose a customer is waiting for information, while the staff members search the system for data. They cannot find it, but they know it's there somewhere. The data is in the system, but it's under a definition in which the staff members are not likely to search. Therefore, in effect, it is unavailable to them. The customer is getting impatient; after all, how difficult can it be to find a small piece of information?

Another example: A state government has multiple divisions within a particular department. Each division has a number of computer systems with multiple databases on these systems. In an effort to make all these databases available to everyone, the data is stored in a data warehouse. When someone wants to print a report, they pull information from the data warehouse. That's where the problems begin.

A manager uses this database to populate reports. He hires a full-time programmer who, in part, has to ensure that the data that employees pull from the warehouse is what they expect it to be. For example, two departments may have datasets with the same name in the data warehouse, or the same label for completely different data records. When they pull a report, they have to make sure they are getting the information that they expect; that it's coming from the right database, the right record, and that it's accurate.

Suggestions for eliminating this type of waste:

— Standardize data definitions.

— Ensure the staff has a ready reference of data fields and definitions.

Data Discrepancies

This type of waste occurs when the same data drawn from the same source at different times is different.

For example, suppose you draw data from a source, and you deliver a report. Then, a day, a week, or a month later, you draw exactly the same data from exactly the same source, but it's different. This causes confusion, it erodes trust in the data, and then someone is left with the task of going back and figuring out which of the values is correct. Data discrepancies suggest a number of things, including data security issues, laxity in error corrections, and so on.

Suggestions for eliminating this type of waste:

— Find the source of the discrepancy: It may not be from within your own organization. In some cases, data discrepancy can occur due to faults not related to the organization—for instance, in cases involving external sources of information.

— To prevent discrepancies arising from within your organization, ensure that the procedures for gathering and storing information are well defined and clearly understood.

— Update all information to make sure it's accurate going forward.

— Set organization-wide standards for information sources.

Process Waste

The most commonly discussed wastes in the context of lean are those occurring in the manufacturing processes. Taiichi Ohno, the pioneer of the Toyota Production System, identified seven types of *muda* (the Japanese word for waste) inherent in all manufacturing processes:

1. Defects

2. Overproduction

3. Inventory

4. Extra processing

5. Motion

6. Waiting

7. Transportation

Over time, lean practitioners added more waste categories to this list.

Manifestations of each of these types can be found in the nonmanufacturing environment, as well. Figure 2-2 lists some of the general types of process-related flaws that can impede the flow of value, and the following sections describe each in more detail, with suggestions for how to prevent and/or eliminate each type of waste.

---

1   Defects
2. Scrap
3. Rework
4. Workarounds
5. Inspecting, checking, and double-checking
6. Approvals
7. Variable flow in a process
8. Too much inventory
9. Incomplete work
10. Overproduction
11. Waiting
12. Overprocessing

Figure 2-2. Types of process waste

Defects

Waste occurs when there is something wrong with the product or service; or it does not serve the purpose for which it was created.

Defects constitute a conspicuous form of process waste. A process defect is one that results in errors or need for rework. Defects can occur due to lapses in the process, inefficient people involved in production or service delivery, or inadequate materials. Many times, the "maker" of the defect is not aware that he or she is producing the defect. The defect is "hidden" until later in the process, or until the customer discovers it.

Defects actually represent two wastes in one—the cost of the defective process or product, and the cost of fixing it. Defects result in increased lead time and order loss, for example, software that does not work under certain conditions, or a delivery service that fails to deliver what is promised. For example, suppose you need to purchase a new washing machine. You go to the Web site of a long-standing retailer whose washing machine rates well in consumer reviews. What the consumer ratings did *not* show you, however, was the delivery experience. You need to make six calls to both the delivery and the service departments to successfully complete the installation. In this case, the defect appears to be systemic. The employees may be doing their best in a system where the processes are complicated, redundant, and inflexible. Aside from your level of frustration, that retailer wastes money sending both service and delivery trucks to your house on several occasions. They should have only had to come out once.

Suggestions for eliminating this type of waste:

There are numerous lean strategies for mistake proofing, some of which are discussed in Chapter 3. The essence of all these strategies is to prevent, rather than eliminate, a defect and nip an error in the bud if it occurs at all.

— To prevent defects, you may need to set in motion a chain of waste-elimination activities. For instance, an inquiry into the cause of a flawed service leads to defects somewhere down the value stream; analysis of this defect reveals more problems, and so on.

— Track down the root cause of the defect, which helps eliminate the possibility of the error being repeated.

Scrap

This is waste because it's leftover material or data that will go unused.

Scrap is inherent to certain processes and products. For example, suppose you advertise for a vacancy in your marketing department—for a job that promises the best career growth and remuneration in the industry. Hundreds or even thousands of applications will likely pour in, from which you ultimately select one candidate. The remaining applications end up as scrap.

Suggestions for eliminating this type of waste:

— It may not always be possible to eliminate scrap altogether, but you could look at recycling or other innovative ways to use it—if not in the same process, maybe elsewhere. For example, you may have created content for a presentation that was cancelled. In some instances it may be worthwhile to archive the content for possible use in other presentations.

— Make any surplus or unused data available to other departments before discarding—it may just be the information for which someone else has been looking. An applicant rejected by marketing may just be the perfect candidate for a position in Human Resources.

— Also consider reducing scrap by including certain controls in the process. In the previous example, making certain qualifications or experience mandatory can limit the number of applicants—and therefore the number of résumés you need to sort through, whether your sorting process is manual or automated with résumé-scanning software.

— Establish clear and specific requirements for a product or service outcome to further reduce scrap.

Rework

This is redoing a task to correct an error. Rework is a consequence of defective processes or service delivery. There are numerous possible sources of defects:

- poor quality control systems
- flawed design
- insufficient training and orientation of employees
- lack of understanding of customer requirements, and so on

Preventing the occurrence of defects should be the priority. Redoing work is almost always nothing but pure waste.

Suggestions for eliminating this type of waste:

— Prevent the waste of rework by preventing the occurrence of defects.

— Keep in mind that the same solutions that apply to defects hold true for rework (see defects section).

Workarounds

This type of waste involves a problem with or obstacle in the system, so using the "official" process does not work. Workarounds are devised in order to get the job done—like cutting the Gordian knot instead of trying to untie it.

Taking a detour from standardized procedures can involve enormous waste of time, effort, and other resources. Workarounds do not guarantee results, and they can never be a long-term solution. In certain cases, they may create legal or quality issues. Moreover, a workaround is merely a quick fix that covers up the real problem. Removing the bottlenecks, however complex they may be, is worth the effort.

Suggestions for eliminating this type of waste:

— Recognize that workarounds are often necessitated by process inefficiencies and poor standardization.

— Compile a set of best practices that includes viable alternatives to standard procedures: This can reduce the need for resorting to workarounds and trial-and-error solutions.

Inspecting, Checking, and Double-checking

These activities validate that the work has been done correctly, but they're still wasteful.

Certain processes build in the need for repeated verifications. It may also be the result of a "tall" organizational hierarchy—one that involves a number of reporting levels. Double-checking invariably increases the lead time and often leads to confusion resulting from a lack of common understanding regarding standards and expectations.

Suggestions for eliminating this type of waste:

— Build checks and balances into the system: This is an efficient alternative to inspecting and checking after the fact.

— Simultaneously, empower each rung in your hierarchy with appropriate accountability and decision making.

Approvals

These are wasteful if they're required to allow standard work to proceed. Although there are exceptions, approvals for a standard process may suggest several possibilities. Among them are the following:

- an opportunity to delegate decision-making authority

- a need for employee training

- a process that generates errors

A standard process should be self-regulating, self-correcting, and at best mistake proofed. When it is not, approvals are required.

Suggestions for eliminating this type of waste:

— Determine why the approval is required. In some cases, approvals may be mandatory due to legal requirements.

— In all other cases, see if the decision making can be effectively delegated. This includes making sure that the standards are communicated to, and owned by, staff members at all levels in the business.

Study the types or errors that occur in the process, and develop solutions to eliminate the errors. Eliminate redundant steps in the approval cycle. Studies show that the greater the number of people involved in approving, the less each individual is likely to assume responsibility for checking and verification.[5]

Variable Flow

This type of waste presents as high peaks and low valleys in production rates. Variable flow can show up as periods of high overtime, punctuated by lulls in production. Although variable flow may be consciously applied to adjust business activity to demand or availability of resources, unplanned fluctuations can strain the entire business process and lead to huge inefficiencies.

A common issue that companies face is closing month-end books and generating reports based on the data. For example, the workers in the finance department of one client consistently worked overtime to meet the schedule.

Because they had been dealing with this process challenge for as long as they could remember, it seemed "normal" to them. Their challenge was to find ways to improve their work flow.

Suggestions for eliminating this type of waste:

— Recognize that variations can occur, not only among time periods, but also among employees and different departments.

— When scheduling work, try to distribute work evenly with all resources— time, labor, equipment, etc.—in mind.

— Use standard processes and templates.

— Reduce redundancies and hand-offs.

Too Much Inventory

Too much physical inventory consumes space. Too much inventory also hides problems in the process, compensating for process errors rather than allowing the problem to surface and addressing the root cause of the problem. Work-in-process (WIP) can impede cash flow and result in longer lead times. Inventory in an office environment may include physical or nonphysical inventory like orders, items waiting for processing, and e-mail.

The just-in-time approach to inventory management, used in manufacturing environments and production processes, helps minimize waste in the form of inventory and work-in-process. Receiving parts from vendors just when they are required helps a firm avoid costs for warehousing. Working on and completing just the right number of parts that are required and can be handled at a given point in time by the next process, helps reduce waste in work-in-process. Achieving this involves aligning production and purchasing to actual demand.

Too much information in "inventory" is also a waste. Apply the just-in-time principle here, too. How? When conducting lean training, for example, try to conduct the training at the time that the knowledge will be used—just-in-time. This accomplishes two things:

1. It solidifies the learning with practical application.

2. It reduces the amount of time that is spent forgetting what was learned.

Suggestions for eliminating this type of waste:

— Document the requirements for each step of the process.

— Provide only what is needed by the downstream process, at a rate that the downstream process can handle.

Incomplete Work

This type of waste obviously refers to work that has stopped midway for any reason. Incomplete work is a subcategory of inventory. The reasons for incomplete work may include the following:

- cancellation of the work originally requested

- a change in management

- interruption by or objection from an internal or external source

- in certain situations—for instance, when there is a major change in strategy and objectives—it may be in the best interest of the organization to discontinue a process midway

Suggestions for eliminating this type of waste:

— Weigh the pros and cons of leaving a process incomplete before making a final decision.

— Determine the reason for the interruption in the work flow, and move to resolve that.

Overproduction

Quite simply, this is waste because you're producing more of something than is actually needed at the time.

Overproduction presents as inventory. In the office environment, inventory shows up as accumulation of work; be it physical like paperwork, or virtual like information waiting its turn to be processed (certain e-mails in the in-box, for example). Work orders printed ahead of time are a common example of overproduction. Another form of overproduction is the generation of unnecessary data. Overproduction signals other process issues such as process bottlenecks, poor feedback loops, training issues, and batch processing.

Suggestions for eliminating this type of waste:

— Recognize that overproduction is the result of other types of wastes in the aforementioned process.

— Resolve those issues (i.e., process bottlenecks, poor feedback loops, training issues, or batch processing), which will automatically ensure that production is aligned with demand.

Waiting

Waiting for something to happen is another form of waste—for instance, waiting for some data or for someone else to complete work.

For example, suppose you have completed an important proposal that has to go to the head office. Just when you try to e-mail it, your Internet access breaks down. Now you have to wait until the next day—a delay that could possibly cost you a major order or sale or an employee, depending on the type of proposal. Wasteful waiting periods can result from any or all of the following problems:

- unbalanced workload

- inefficiencies in automation

- poor planning and scheduling

- improper communication

Suggestions for eliminating this type of waste:

— Balance the workload by redistributing tasks along the process flow.

— Establish a "pull" system.

— Remove unnecessary approval processes.

— Build multiple tasks into daily work schedules, to ensure that employees are productively occupied even during waiting periods.

— Prevent delays due to problems in automation by providing for backups and "standard workarounds."

Overprocessing

This is extra processing that is not really necessary to get the job done, and does not add any value.

Often, many processes or activities are continued as a habit or made routine even when they have lost their relevance. For instance, an office may keep its tradition of daily or weekly meetings, even when no specific reason can justifies them. Another common example is the practice of printing out receipts even when the customer may not require them. Additional steps in the process not only take more time, but also provide additional opportunities to generate errors.

Suggestions for eliminating this type of waste:

— Implement advances in technology that can often shorten and simplify processes.

— Examine your office processes at regular intervals to spot any redundancies or flab.

— Conduct external benchmarking to discover more efficient work procedures.

— Actively seek suggestions from employees and customers for simplifying work and eliminating unnecessary steps.

Physical Environment Waste

Two types of waste often found in the physical environment are:

1. Waste related to safety

2. Waste related to the movement of people or objects

The next sections describe each of these in more detail, with suggestions on how to prevent and/or eliminate each type of waste.

Safety

A safe physical environment is one where all workers are protected from harm. Unfortunately, safety in the office environment does not draw the attention that it does in the factory.

Many safety issues arise in an office environment. A partial list includes the following:

- poor ventilation

- insufficient lighting

- noise

- fire hazards

- faulty office furniture

- the use of chairs and tables as ladders

- unbalanced file cabinets or unsecured shelving prone to tipping

- trip hazards, such as electrical cords or computer cables

- ergonomic issues

Office safety needs to be addressed because injuries in the office environment also cost money in lost productivity and compensation. Attending to office safety not only improves productivity, but also sends a message that you care about employees.

Suggestions for eliminating this type of waste:

— Although safety issues are frequently ergonomic, to maintain a healthy office environment, also pay attention to the following:

- chemical hazards, equipment, and workstation design

- the physical environment (temperature, humidity, light, noise, ventilation, cleanliness, and space)

- task design

- psychological factors (personal interactions, work pace, job control)

— Make sure your office diligently adheres to safety laws and regulations.

— For additional detailed information on office safety, consult the National Institute for Occupational Safety and Health: http://www.cdc.gov/niosh/topics/officeenvironment/officeenvironment.html

Movement

Waste in the physical environment can also occur when people are moving or physical items are being transported from one place to another in the office.

Wastes in the form of movement often results from flaws in workplace design. Movement waste occurs when there is physical distance between adjacent process steps. For example, in the scheduling and billing process referred to earlier in this chapter, the production scheduler, who interfaced with customers, had to walk more than 1,000 feet to deliver a work order to a production planner, who managed the actual production flow. Not only did the movement take time, but the distance created a batch flow—the production scheduler would accumulate several work orders before making the trip to the planner's office. This also delayed the planner's knowledge of what new orders were in the system.

Other types of movement waste, which have become an almost integral part of office work, include walking to a centrally located printer or fax machine and traveling—often, across countries or continents—for meetings and discussions.

Suggestions for eliminating this type of waste:

— Minimize the amount of moving, walking, or other forms of transport. For example, keep work-related materials within reach, and group together materials, equipment, technology, and people at the workstation.

— To reduce flow of paper, keep "hard copies" to a minimum.

— Locate tasks next to each other whenever possible.

People Waste

Human capital is undoubtedly the most valuable asset of any business; it is also probably the only asset that is unique and irreplaceable. Consequently, wastes related to human resources can prove costly for the business.

As with most concepts in human resources management, the wastes related to people are often abstract and difficult to pinpoint. Figure 2-3 lists those most likely to show up in a kaizen event, and the next sections describe them in more detail, with suggestions on how to prevent and/or eliminate each type.

1. Unclear role (unclear responsibility, authority, and accountability)
2. Lack of training
3. Work or task interruptions
4. Multitasking
5. Underutilization of talent
6. Hierarchy and structure
7. Recruitment errors
8. Lack of strategic focus

Figure 2-3. Types of people waste

Unclear Role (Unclear Responsibility, Authority, and Accountability)

This type of waste involves the lack of clarity regarding any or all of the following:

- What an individual or organization is responsible for doing

- What is included and not included in the job

- The boundaries of an employee's authority

- To whom the individual or organization is accountable

The impact of unclear roles can range from *no one* assuming responsibility for a task, to more than one person (or group) *competing* for responsibility for the same task. When the responsibility, authority, or accountability for a role is unclear, a number of impediments may occur, including clashes among groups or individuals, tentative behavior, and duplication of efforts, to name just a few. Ambiguity in role definitions also causes delays and interruptions in work, because it makes it easier for people to "pass the buck."

For example, the sales manager of a consumer goods company outlines an exciting new strategy that involves recruiting a number of new sales executives. Simultaneously, *but separately*, the sales director and the HR function work together on job analysis and performance data and decide to *reduce* the sales force. This could have been avoided by clarifying the responsibility for sales strategy. (Improving the level of involvement of stakeholders would have helped in this situation, also.)

Suggestions for eliminating this type of waste:

- Resolve role and task ambiguities through in-depth job analysis.

- Clarify all job descriptions.

- Make sure you have a well-defined organizational structure.

- Facilitate communication across hierarchical and functional levels.

Lack of Training

This type of waste includes both insufficient job-related training and developmental training.

The future belongs to the learning organization. You need to update the skills and knowledge of your people, and enable them to acquire new competencies in response to changing business needs. Failure to train your employees regularly and properly can deprive your company of the competitive edge. Lack of appropriate training often results in other types of waste such as defects and delays.

Suggestions for eliminating this type of waste:

— Analyze the skills and knowledge necessary to successfully perform each job, and make sure that the people doing it have those skills. For instance, with the IT revolution and computerization, employees responsible for tasks that have been computerized will need additional training.

— Recognize that a change for the better in any process will entail training employees in the new system to capture its full potential.

— Consider a proactive alternative to remedy lack of training: Recruit people having all competencies required for a particular job. Of course, this does not eliminate the need for continuous training and development—a "training culture" should be part of the organization's strategy.

Interruptions

This type of waste occurs when someone focused on a particular task is unexpectedly diverted to another task or issue, leaving the task unfinished.

Phone calls, e-mails requiring urgent attention, unplanned meetings—interruptions seem to be a fixture in the modern office environment. Some interruptions are a product of process design—or the lack of it. Interruptions lower the quality of work, requiring mental setup time when the individual returns to the task. So, how can a process be designed to eliminate interruptions?

Here's one example of a company that dealt with interruptions. Five employees were responsible for receiving and stocking product. They were also responsible for taking customer calls on the phone. When processing a product, they were frequently interrupted by phone calls from customers. While they were able to respond immediately to customer calls, the receiving and stocking process suffered. In fact, it was impossible to get accurate productivity measures on the receiving/stocking process because of the phone interruptions.

To eliminate the interruptions, the managers assigned two of the employees to take customer calls, and the other three worked on receiving. They rotated the roles so that everyone did both customer calls and receiving/stocking. This accomplished several things for them and their processes:

• It allowed standard work for the receiving/stocking process.

• It made collecting metrics and improving that process easier.

- It reduced the amount of "mental setup" time required upon return to the receiving/stocking process after an interruption.

- The team was still able to give call-in customers immediate attention.

Suggestions for eliminating this type of waste:

— To some extent, you can eliminate interruptions through proper planning, scheduling, and prioritization of work.

— Make sure you encourage such planning, scheduling, and prioritization of work at all levels: the individual, department, and the organization as a whole.

— Have managers delegate appropriate decision-making authority to capable employees.

Multitasking

Waste often occurs when people intentionally conduct more than one task simultaneously—when they can't really handle more than one at a time.

Individuals with the ability to perform more than one task at a time are valued in the current competitive environment. They are often required to "do more with less," so multitasking becomes an intentional or inadvertent survival skill. Organizations may use multitasking to make the most efficient use of human resources. Herein lies the danger—multitasking can become counterproductive. Although some people are better than others at multitasking, even those who excel at it can slow down and increase the likelihood of quality errors. Waste results from the mental setup time it takes to shift from one task to another, or to do two or more tasks simultaneously.[6] It is also difficult to track actual productivity against a task when the task is punctuated by interruptions.

Suggestions for eliminating this type of waste:

— Rather than multitask across all jobs, decide which approach best suits each process, role, or work area.

— If multitasking is a competency required for a particular role, keep that skill in mind at the point of recruitment.

— Ensure that separate targets, standards, and metrics are applied to each task.

Underutilization of talent

Waste occurs when the productive or creative potential of human resources is not fully utilized.

Unleashing the full potential of an individual is not easy. Often, the individual, is not fully aware of his or her competencies. Successful organizations take concrete steps to ensure that their employees are fully utilized. Underutilization of human resources can occur in many forms, such as:

- A person may be limited by the boundaries of her job description and therefore does not get the opportunity to contribute creatively.

- A business culture may discourage innovation.

- The culture may indulge in organizational politics.

- The culture may maintain archaic reporting systems with no scope of empowerment for the lower levels.

- The business may discourage cross-functional exposure (i.e., to different types of work functions in the organization).

All of these scenarios will create and spawn this unfortunate and massive type of waste.

Suggestions for eliminating this type of waste:

- Build value for human capital needs into the organization's culture.

- Make sure your leadership is open to suggestions and ideas from all levels.

- Give employees a chance to perform in other functions, levels, and geographies, whenever possible.

- Encourage employees to have an active say in performance appraisals and career planning.

- Use empowerment techniques, such as the formation of self-directed teams, to contribute significantly toward utilizing the potential of every employee.

Hierarchy and Structure

Waste also occurs if an organization's structure is multilayered, so that the presence of unnecessary vertical layers impedes the flow of value.

The purpose of having hierarchical levels is to ensure that accountability is distributed according to the importance or complexity of a task. However, a vertically tall organizational structure is detrimental to the smooth flow of value. It creates unnecessary processes and complicates the approval system, thus lengthening the lead time.

Another costly and more intrinsic form of waste occurs when people at the lowest levels are isolated from the organization's strategic objectives and vision. In firms with this kind of hierarchy, empowerment levels are typically low, resulting in poor motivation and low employee engagement. A structure that is not flat results in waste of ideas and potential, because the voice of those in the lower rungs is seldom communicated to the people who make strategic decisions.

Suggestions for eliminating this type of waste:

— Facilitate smooth and efficient flow of value by requiring top-down as well as bottom-up channels of communication.

— Keep in mind that, although an absolutely flat organization may be a Utopian concept, it is not difficult to ensure that all employees are involved in strategic planning and goal setting.

— Delegate responsibility and entrust every employee with some level of decision making, to accelerate the process and inculcate a sense of ownership.

Recruitment Errors

This type of waste occurs when an organization selects the wrong person, or loses out on the right person, for a job.

Recruitment costs and payroll form some of the biggest expenses for most organizations. Errors in selection can result in huge and often long-term wastes to the organization and to the individual. Wastes can occur from two kinds of recruitment error:

1. Type I errors occur when the recruiters overlook a candidate who would have been the "perfect fit." This is a form of unutilized talent.

2. A more serious recruitment error is Type II—when the wrong candidate is recruited. This can occur due to flaws in job description, lack of proper competency mapping and job analysis, use of inappropriate recruitment methods, and lack of recruitment skills.

Suggestions for eliminating this type of waste:

— When conducting job and competency analyses, include inputs from all stake-holders—top management, current role holders, peers in other departments, customers, and so on.

— Make sure the recruitment panel also includes representatives from all concerned functions.

— Customize the criteria and tools used for recruitment to the role, profile of candidates, department, and level.

Lack of Strategic Focus

This type of waste occurs when people work in silos, without focusing on organizational goals (i.e., they focus only on the goals of their specific department, division, or work group), and creating an internal conflict of interest.

Conflicts of interests are a common form of people waste in modern organizations. For example, a manager may want to recruit more people, but the finance department feels it's time to cut down on people costs. At an individual level, people focus on "urgent but unimportant" tasks and lose sight of broader, long-term priorities.

Another result from a lack of strategic focus is departmental projects that do not contribute advancement toward achieving business goals. Projects should be aligned with the larger business strategy.

Suggestions for eliminating this type of waste:

— Align individual and department goals and projects to the organizational strategy.

— Let every employee participate in strategic planning.

— Be transparent about the long-term objectives, mission, and vision of your organization as a whole.

— Encourage interactions and team building among different departments.

WHAT DO YOU DO WITH WASTE?

Now that you have learned about the different types of waste in an office or service environment, how do you deal with it in your own workplace? Lean offers a number of tools and methods to fight waste and boost productivity. What follows in Chapter 3 is a discussion on how to apply these methods to eliminate waste from business processes and help value flow.

NOTES

1. Don Tapping and Tom Shuker, Value Stream Management for the Lean Office: Eight Steps to Planning, Mapping, and Sustaining Lean Improvements in Administrative Areas, (New York, Productivity Press, 2003), 1.

2. John Y. Lee, "JIT Works for Services Too," CMA Magazine, 1990, volume 64, number 6, 20-23.

3. Thomas A. Fabrizio and Don Tapping, 5S for the Office: Organizing the Workplace to Eliminate Waste, (New York, Productivity Press, 2006), 5.

4. Anonymous, The New Improvement Frontier: Developing Lean Administration, Strategic Direction; 2005,volume 21, number 11, 33-35.

5. "Applying Lean and Reducing Waste," www.idea.gov.uk/idk/aio/4645556

6. Joshua S. Rubinstein, David E. Meyer, Jeffrey E. Evans, "Executive Control of Cognitive Processes in Task Switching," Journal of Experimental Psychology: Human Perception and Performance, 2001, volume 27, number 4, 763-797.

CHAPTER 3

ELEVEN METHODS OF DISCOVERING AND OPTIMIZING VALUE IN THE OFFICE

One of the key benefits that most businesses aspire to gain by implementing lean is the elimination of waste. Today, businesses are vying with one another like never before to win over customers and investors, and to gain a competitive advantage. Against this backdrop, firms are waking up to the need for rooting out inefficiencies from the organization and streamlining all their business processes.

As discussed in Chapter 2, wastes in the front office and administrative processes may be less visible compared with those on the shop floor. However, the results of waste in the office—such as delayed response to customer orders or incorrect accounting—can be costly and often devastating. It is estimated that office processes account for up to 80% of the lead time in many manufacturing and service industries. Thus, purging the office of wastes hastens the journey toward cost-effectiveness, customer satisfaction, and profitability.

There are several approaches to reducing waste and streamlining business operations for maximizing value. Although each approach addresses the issue of waste from a distinct perspective, they all strive to achieve certain fundamental objectives of lean—such as reduction in cost and time, improving the flow of information, and optimizing value. Figure 3-1 is a partial list of the numerous principles and methods used by lean practitioners.

The key lean concepts that are most useful to an organization when setting out on a lean journey include the following:

1. The 5Ss	7. Takt time
2. Visual control	8. Pitch
3. Continuous flow	9. Workload leveling
4. Mistake proofing	10. Pull
5. Standard operations	11. Work cells
6. Just-in-time	

Figure 3-1: Key lean concepts

These eleven methods address most of the common issues that new imple-menters face. Many of these concepts are far reaching, and to fully explore them would exceed the boundaries of this book, but this chapter provides an overview. (For more information on these concepts, visit www.strausforest.com and www.productivitypress.com.)

METHOD #1: 5S

The abbreviation "5S" stands for *sort, simplify, sweep, standardize*, and *sustain*. 5S is an approach to "housekeeping" that frees up physical, virtual, and men-tal space. Many types of waste in the office—such as defects, movement, unavailable data, and waiting—arise from poor organization of processes and the physical workspace. The aim of the 5Ss is to clear up clutter and create a clean, safe, organized workplace that is conducive to the open and smooth flow of value. It is usually recommended as the first step in the lean journey because it clarifies the task at hand, making improvements easier to identify and imple-ment. Figure 3-2 provides a quick overview of the goal of each phase, and the next sections describe each phase in more detail.

Activity	Description
Sort	Identify and separate elements required for the task
Simplify	Simplify the process and workspace
Sweep	Remove unnecessary items
Standardize	Document the process
Sustain	Maintain the changes

Figure 3-2: 5S in the Office

Phase 1: Sort

In this first phase of 5S, the task is to sort through the process environment, separating the *necessary* from the *unnecessary* elements within the process. Through this sorting, you should end up with only the essentials and impera-tives to complete the job. In the office setup, an innumerable amount of tiny tasks consume time, increase complexity, and foster unnecessary resource uti-lization. They seem so vital, until the firm decides to get lean. Here are just a few examples:

- Duplication of information resulting in more paperwork and files

- Multiple approval forms that must wait until all relevant parties have signed

- Multiple levels of checking (automated as well as manual) for a task that should create an error-free product the first time (this is another scenario that should be highlighted in this phase.)

Phase 2: Simplify

In the next phase, *simplify*, you look for ways to simplify your processes and your work space. Unnecessary complexity is common in office environments. This may stem, for example, from workarounds or old processes that have not been updated to match current conditions.

Complexity in the physical environment can also result from disorganized workplaces. Removing clutter and organizing objects, processes, and space in a user-friendly manner is the essence of the second stage. It involves putting everything in place, creating transparency, and ensuring that objects and information are easily accessible to everyone concerned.

Phase 3: Sweep

The *sweep* phase involves removing, eliminating, or archiving things identified as not process-necessary in the *sort* and *simplify* phases. This includes cleaning up in a physical sense, as well as cleaning up processes and systems to maximize efficiency. The idea is to maintain the workplace, equipment, and processes in a productive and ready-to-use condition.

Phase 4: Standardize

Once the business process is sorted, simplified, and swept, the next step is to *standardize* and document best practices. This calls for a definition of what is normal and expected. Unless you standardize and document the improved processes, you are likely to revert to old ways and lose the benefits you have gained.

As far as possible, involve all concerned employees in formulating the standards so that you do not miss out on any valuable perspective or experience. The documented standards should be easy to understand, and should be communicated across all relevant levels and functions.

Phase 5: Sustain

The last step, *sustain*, involves following the first four Ss on a continuous basis so as to foster a disciplined culture of practicing the 5Ss in the organization. It includes the following:

- Training all employees in implementing the changes

- Monitoring the improvements

- Transforming the organizational mindset to ensure that things do not return to *status quo*

Sustaining 5S activities creates a solid foundation upon which to build improvements later on.

Applying the 5Ss in the Information Domain

The 5Ss can be applied to computer desktops, e-mails, hard drives, and so on. For instance, time spent searching for a specific file or e-mail is time wasted on nonproductive activities. When 5S-ing information, here are some considerations:

- Review company policy and legal requirements before deleting files and e-mails. You may be required to archive certain kinds of information.

- Since memory and storage space is shrinking in size and cost, the convenience of having archived files available for reference or reuse may outweigh the value of deleting them.

- Search-engine technology may change the rules for keeping or deleting electronic files. The ability to search vast numbers of files quickly increases the potential value of archiving information.

In the physical world, it may make sense to put physical documents in a labeled file folder, which goes into a labeled hanging folder in a particular labeled file cabinet. Clutter on the desktop may also be eliminated. Material, tools, and information should be readily available and accessible.

Make sure filenames are consistent or that old e-mails are properly archived or deleted. The use of consistent, standardized filenames in consistent, standardized locations supports productivity and continuous improvement, just like it does on the physical desktop with an inbox or file cabinet.

Proper implementation of the 5Ss not only enhances productivity, but also boosts employee morale and creates a sense of belonging toward work and the workplace.

METHOD #2: VISUAL CONTROLS

A "visual workplace" is an integral element of the lean philosophy. Visual controls are feedback systems that tell workers and management the current state of the work system. For example:

- In call centers, this may be a reader board on the wall or on the computer screen that displays the number of calls in queue, average wait times, current call time, and other similar metrics. Figure 3-3 shows a sample reader board with these metrics.

Figure 3-3: Sample reader board

- In a purchasing office, visual controls might be a board that indicates how many orders have yet to be placed, how many are behind, and how many are past due.

- Signal boards in banks and post offices that flash the "token" number currently being serviced is another ubiquitous visual control.

The advantage of visual controls is that, at a glance, they provide everyone with critical information about how work is progressing. This information allows people to respond quickly to any issues that may arise. In effect, visual controls empower employees by making the workplace and processes self-explanatory.

METHOD #3: CONTINUOUS FLOW

Continuous flow, or one-piece flow, is the condition where a product, service, or an element progresses through the value stream without interruption. In manufacturing, it implies that one part is processed at a time and completed before flowing to the next stage. In offices, continuous flow involves completing each process accurately and without interruptions.

The relationship between continuous flow and waste reduction is a chicken-or-egg paradox. Establishing continuous flow eliminates waste, but reduction of waste is a prerequisite for maintaining continuous flow. In a process riddled with waste, the application of one-piece flow can cause delays and long wait-ing periods, and in fact, become counterproductive. Hence, both aspects need to be addressed simultaneously.

Continuous Flow in an Office Environment

Instituting continuous flow in the office environment is a challenge. Customer responsiveness is *the* issue for many service industries. However, constant interruption is an inherent quality of many offices. Phone calls and e-mails constantly interrupt people and their work. Demands may come from many directions. For example, managers are often called to respond to competing organizational stakeholders. Top management requires information to make important business decisions, and that information needs to be present at the end of day. Simultaneously, employees await the manager's attention to solve problems or make decisions that they are ill-equipped or unauthorized to do.

Some of this cannot be changed, and the management function may always be issue-driven, but working toward continuous flow can still be beneficial. To start with, a manager can reduce the interruptions flowing from those report-ing to him or her by effectively delegating decision-making authority where it makes sense. This frees time to focus on important business issues.

Another option is to bucket tasks where there is a bottleneck and tackle those immediately. The other tasks (independent deliverables) can be handled through effective time management by, for example, setting aside a specific time to deal with phone calls or e-mails, or planning for the day. Again, situations within individual organizations may differ, requiring customized solutions.

For example, one manager recaptured 40 hours per month by delegating tasks to her direct reports. Some of the tasks she delegated included managing e-mail for the department, handling product returns, managing special orders, and managing inventory. By off-loading this work to her employees, she had more time to spend her energy on business development. Her employees appre-ciated the new responsibilities, adding another positive by-product.

A prerequisite to establishing successful continuous flow is effective com-munication and cooperation among the various processes. In fact, emphasis on continuous flow promotes cooperation among employees by highlighting the symbiotic aspect of their relationship. This encourages teamwork and group accountability.

For example, in an office scenario, divisional accountants or clerks compile weekly or monthly statistics and send them to the company accountant. He then collates the information to provide holistic companywide statistics to pre-sent to the board of directors. This period is usually a harrying time for all the accountants, as they rush around preparing tables and charts; some that will be used in the final report and others that will gather dust. Effective communication between them would not only reduce waste, but also reduce stress. Most important, they will start working with each other rather than working at (or worse, against) each other.

METHOD #4: MISTAKE PROOFING

"If something can go wrong, it will," states Murphy's law. The intention of mistake proofing, or poka yoke (as it is known in Japanese), is to make it impossible, or at least difficult, to commit errors. Defects are the most common form of waste in both manufacturing and office situations. Mistake proofing frees up valuable time, increases reliability, cuts cost, and improves overall productivity. Poka yoke is not about simply correcting a mistake. It involves tracing and eliminating the root cause of the mistake.

Mistake proofing in the nonphysical office can be challenging, but it's worth the effort. It's especially effective in repetitive tasks, which involve attention to detail or memorization, and hence hold high potential for mistakes. One example of mistake proofing is designing fields on a Web document that will not allow the user to continue unless these fields are filled out in a particular way. For example, the Internal Revenue Service uses online forms that generate error messages if fields are left blank or if unexpected data is put into a particular form field. Although this does not necessarily prevent the wrong information from being entered, it does block blank entries or incorrect data formats.

Another way to mistake proof online forms, is to make them simple and user-friendly with clear, intuitive instructions. The field of usability design has generated valuable knowledge on how to design information interfaces for maximum productivity.

Other common examples of mistake-proofing tools in nonmanufacturing settings are the devices in retail stores that beep if products are removed from the store before scanning, thus preventing theft. Another example: an ATM that flashes a signal and beeps after ejecting the ATM card. In a paper-and-file office, color-coded forms that go into files of the same color ensure that everything is in its right place.

METHOD #5: STANDARD OPERATIONS

A phrase often heard among lean consultants is "without standard operations, there is no kaizen." Standard operations, in lean and the 5Ss, involve more than documenting a particular way of doing a task or series of tasks. Instead, standard operations mean following the documented way of doing things, day in and day out.

If the system is in constant flux because of variations in how work is done, it becomes difficult to monitor and maintain the effects of change. Standardized work provides a *stable framework* for identifying problem areas and making improvements. It ensures that all work is done in the same, and best possible, manner. This reduces variation in outcomes, increases reliability, and enables optimum utilization of available resources.

Standard operations are not cast in concrete, and they should change as a result of subsequent improvements to the process. It is important to remember that *standardization does not hinder creativity*. Standardization of work is a dynamic process that facilitates continuous improvement. The best practices should include inputs from all employees, and these practices should be evaluated and modified on a regular basis. Ideally, in the current competitive business scenario, standards should be based on industry-wide, cross-industry, and global benchmarks.

The documented version of standard operations, sometimes called standard work, consists of:

- the rate of customer demand (or takt time, explained in Method #7)

- the process steps

- the amount of work that should be in the system at any particular time

Often, this is represented as a standard work chart. For office processes, standard work can include the right sequence of activities in performing a job and the time required to perform each activity. Another application of standardization is a competency map that depicts competencies required for a certain level or role across functions, departments, and even geographies. This helps to prevent staffing errors involving recruitment of candidates without the requisite skills.

METHOD #6: JUST-IN-TIME

Just-in-time (JIT) is a strategy implemented to eliminate the sources of manufacturing waste, by reducing the work-in-process (WIP) inventory and its associated costs. Just-in-time enables the internal processes of an organization to adapt to sudden changes in demand by producing the *right product* at the *right time*, and in the *right quantities*. Just-in-time involves having on hand only enough raw materials, WIP, or finished products required for a smooth operation, and no more.

When existing stock dips to the reorder level, the stock-ordering process is triggered to order the required quantity. Ordering stocks only when needed—in small, frequent lots—saves on warehouse space and costs.

Just-in-time in nonmanufacturing environments addresses the flow and storage of resources—usually data and information. In a data-driven process where data is required to make decisions, it makes no sense to deliver the information to the user before he or she is ready to use it. The information should arrive to the user as he or she is ready to use it, or better yet the user should be able to pull the latest data when he or she is ready.

Another example from the knowledge work environment is the combination of membership and search options on Web sites and e-journals that give you access to information when you need it. This is a JIT alternative to subscribing and receiving all issues of journals. Another instance of JIT on the Internet is the option of bookmarking Web sites, which allows the reader to visit the bookmarked site when he or she wants it, without having to go through the search engine each time or having to permanently load that information onto his or her system. For example, if you frequently buy training materials from one particular online vendor, it makes sense to bookmark that vendor's site.

Just-in-time is not a single tool, but a way of thinking that can be applied to different situations. If implemented well, JIT can lead to dramatic improvements in an organization's efficiency, quality, and return on investment. It saves time, space, and money. More important, JIT ensures that resources—material or human—are utilized to maximum competitive advantage.

METHOD #7: TAKT TIME

Takt is a German word that refers to musical beat or rhythm. In the work environment, the takt time is the time available to produce a product in order to meet customer demand. The pace and alignment of production flow is set using the takt time. Product flow is expected to fall within a pace that is equal to the takt time.

Here is how takt time is calculated:

Takt time = (Available work time per day) / (Customer demand per day)

For instance, if the customer demand is sixteen purchase orders processed per day, and the daily available work time is 8 hours, that is 480 minutes, then the takt time is calculated as 480 ÷ 16 = 30 minutes. This effectively means that one purchase order should be processed through the production system, on average, every 30 minutes.

METHOD #8: PITCH

In the office scenario, takt time can be combined with "pitch" to manage the process time to customer demand. Pitch is the pace and flow of a product grouping, or *pitch increment*.

For instance, consider the purchase order takt time, previously mentioned. Using those defined numbers, the takt time is determined to be 30 minutes, but purchase orders vary in complexity, availability, and a host of other factors. Some orders may take 5 minutes to process, while others may take as long as 1 hour. To minimize variation against takt time, orders are aggregated. In this case, the client chose to establish a pitch of 2 hours. That meant that on average, 4 purchase orders should be processed every 2 hours.

Another practical application of the pitch concept can be illustrated in a call center. In this particular case, a client receives alerts about errors in the support software. Troubleshooting scripts (the information that call-center personnel use to help clients calling in with product problems) contain solutions to the errors, missing information, or information that needs to be updated on clients' products. The support staff receives about 32 alerts every day. To respond to these alerts, it makes sense to calculate how many need to be dealt with per time unit. That would be takt time. Here is the calculation for this case:

480 ÷ 32 = 15

The takt time is 15 minutes. However, the time to resolve errors varies dramatically, depending on the complexity of the issue and the availability of expertise. Some errors may be a simple spelling correction; the solution may be easily available in the script and take 1 hour to resolve; or it may require a more labor-intensive effort to resolve the error—waiting on another group for an answer, for example, and taking 5 hours. In this case, it would make sense to aggregate the takt time over several error alerts to allow for the variability. This helps to smooth out the process metrics, reducing the amplitude of being above or below takt time. This department chose a pitch of 1 hour.

METHOD #9: WORKLOAD LEVELING

Workload leveling or leveled production, referred to in Japanese as *heijunka*, is the process of producing output in a specific uniform cycle to overcome queuing and line stoppage problems, and to match the rate of customer demand. This means that production cycle times at individual work cells are coordinated based on customer demand. Work, therefore, flows smoothly and continuously throughout the entire manufacturing process.

Takt time, the central feature of a lean system, is used to achieve leveled production. Takt time is essential to the smooth flow of work through production cells, and it's a key factor in planning and scheduling work. By using takt time, the production levels can be set into a computer system for any date and duration. Workload leveling results in a steady demand pattern and ensures a predictable, smooth schedule, thus avoiding capacity bottlenecks.

In the office, workload leveling is usually applied to time schedules. Based on the deadline for a major project, time targets can be set for each stage—research, meetings, presentations, initial drafting, pilot studies, and so on. Workload leveling can also be manifested as delegation of work among project teams. Another way of applying workload leveling is to demarcate a certain time for low-priority activities to ensure that critical work and targets do not get negatively affected.

Here's a simple example. A large mail-order pharmacy has an order-entry process that has a number of steps. The process begins with these two steps: enter order, and then verify eligibility. The volume of orders is sufficient to require two employees to keep up with customer demand. In this case, the rate of customer demand, or takt time, is one order per minute. The average time to enter an order takes 45 seconds. The average time to verify eligibility is 1 minute and 15 seconds. The workload is unbalanced because the time to process a claim is unequal between entry and verification. The challenge here is to find a way to balance the workload so that each step takes 1 minute—equal to the rate of customer demand.

METHOD #10: PULL

Pull systems are the key characteristics of a lean, demand-driven production system. A pull system ensures that production and material requirements are based on actual customer demand, rather than relying solely on potentially inaccurate forecasting tools.

In the JIT production process, customer demand is the genesis of the order; it sends the first signal to production. This results in the product getting pulled out of the assembly process. The final assembly line goes to the preceding process and pulls the necessary elements and items in the required quantities. This goes on, as each process pulls the needed parts from the preceding process further upstream. The whole process is coordinated using the kanban system, a means to specify and signal the type and quantity of product to produce. A kanban signal could be a card, a visual aid, or a software-generated signal that triggers the supply, movement, or production of the parts and components.

The ultimate goal of a pull system is to control the flow of materials, by replacing only those items that have been actually consumed in the production process. The pull system eliminates waste by basing new orders on *actual demand* rather than *forecasts*.

Here's how this can play out in an office environment. Suppose your HR department has a team that's recruiting sales supervisors. Each team member handles a different stage of the process and does not send work to the next step until the person doing the next step is ready to take work forward from there. Company policy says that internal applicants should be considered before seeking out external candidates. So one team member scans the internal applications and passes them to the person responsible for interviewing and recruiting. The number of candidates recruited internally is displayed on a chart (or the HR Intranet). Based on this data, the team members in charge of external recruitment begins their process but not before receiving the data.

Why do it this way? One, the fact that work is piling up on a person does not make the work go faster. Two, if there is a work imbalance, the person who is idle can focus on resolving the cause of the problem, whether it means devoting resources to the bottleneck, or improving the bottleneck process.

This step-by-step process often helps eliminate a number of steps or activities, which may be rendered unnecessary by the successful completion of previous steps. The idea is to perform an operation only if there is a pull or demand—be it from internal or external customers. The use of visual signals ensures transparency and, in effect, mistake proofs the communication and coordination process.

METHOD #11: WORK CELLS

A work cell is a group of equipment or people that perform similar work or are responsible for similar outcomes. When applied to the lean office, the work cell concept addresses the issue of work and workplace layout. This refers, not only to the efficient placement of office equipment, but also to the layout of the organizational structure.

In a typical, functional layout, people are grouped together based on divisions or departments. In contrast, a work cell is often a *cross-functional entity*, which includes people responsible for the flow of a particular process or value stream.

The work cell approach offers the following workplace benefits:

- It removes a number of people-related wastes.

- It promotes cooperation.

- It gives employees a holistic perception of their work.

- On the whole, it promotes commitment to organizational goals and strategy.

One client, a group of engineers and illustrators that developed technical publications, was originally located in two different parts of the same building, with the engineers on one floor, and the illustrators on another. After conducting a lean kaizen on their process, the client chose to relocate so that engineers and illustrators sat side by side. Their efficiency and job satisfaction increased.

SOME LEAN SUCCESS STORIES

The tools and techniques discussed in this chapter can be applied to most business processes to facilitate the smooth flow of value. However, it goes without saying, that the application of any, or all, of these methods should be based on a holistic perspective of the process. At any stage of the lean journey, you need to have a clear understanding about where you are, where you want to be, and which route is best suited to your expedition.

Thus, the success of these techniques depends on how well you adapt and blend them to suit your organization's needs, processes, strategy, and so on. Therefore, this chapter concludes with a glimpse of firms—across different industries—that implemented some of the tools and techniques described in this chapter and that reaped remarkable results.

Implementing Lean in a Manufacturing Office

A manufacturer of custom-made, high-performance label and die-cut adhesives applied lean principles to its front office processes, primarily to reduce the lead time from order entry to shipping. It made several modifications to streamline processes and eliminate wasteful practices—for example:

- The order bins were placed close to those responsible for processing.

- The bins were clearly labeled so that all concerned employees would know where to find a particular order.

- In addition, the staff was given cross-functional training.

As a result of these changes, the company has *reduced its process time from 41 hours to 6 hours*. The company has managed a savings of $150,000 in benefits and payroll.[1]

Implementing Lean in an Agricultural Office

A firm that makes and markets fruit confectionery used lean to eliminate waste and streamline its mail-order process. Through kaizen events, managers identified several non-value-adding processes, which were adding to the lead time. Based on their findings, they made the following changes:

- They eliminated the "mail sorter" position and divided the work among other employees.

- Although the company had an electronic mail opener and sorter, it used manual processes simultaneously; with lean, they removed this redundancy.

The intervention helped this company reduce work-in-process by 50%.[2]

Implementing Lean in a Doctor's Office

A family physician achieved something akin to "one-piece flow" in his private practice by analyzing the entire patient process, identifying waste and eliminating it. An electronic health recorder that records patient information and presents it just-in-time to the physician improved the process. All documents, including the prescription, are printed and electronically stored. The doctor has achieved incredible success—the average waiting time for a patient is 63 seconds, and he gets a detailed print report including the diagnosis, prescription, and details of the next appointment within 60 seconds of completing the check-up.[3]

The principles of lean are powerful tools to help you achieve your productivity goals. As you can see from the examples mentioned, gains can be dramatic. However, clarifying your lean improvements is critical to reaching your business objectives. Improving the wrong thing may yield you little.

The next chapter describes a way to help you focus on the right things. Value-stream mapping is a tool to help you understand your current process, to envision your future process, and to plan how to reach that respective goal.

NOTES

1. "Eliminating Waste in the Front Office," *The Business Journal of Milwaukee*, December 15, 2006. http://milwaukee.bizjournals.com/milwaukee /stories/2006/12/18/focus2.html (Page 2)

2. http://www.gemba.com/uploadedFiles/Liberty%20Orchards%20Mail%20 Order%20Process(2).pdf

3. "Patient-Centered Care Supported by EHR," http://kanban.blogspot.com/ 2006/06/amazing-single-piece-flow-md-office.html

CHAPTER 4

MAPPING THE VALUE STREAM IN THE OFFICE

Although this book is not about value-stream mapping, the process itself certainly warrants discussion. It is recommended that you map your value stream before doing an office kaizen, unless your intention is to pilot a kaizen event as a proof of concept. Embarking on a series of lean office kaizens without value-stream mapping your system involves many risks, such as the following:

- Improvement efforts that are not aligned with business strategy

- Random improvements in the process that do not connect into a cohesive result

- Lack of communication and coordination with other elements of the organization

Implementing lean requires high levels of investment and organizational commitment. Expending these resources and energy in a haphazard manner without a clear sense of direction is wasteful and counterproductive. Value-stream mapping provides a unifying plan that helps focus your lean efforts on the process issues that most impact your organization's strategic intentions.

Another risk of doing a lean event without value-stream mapping is generating a series of improvements that do not yield a systemic result. You may indeed have successful process improvement efforts, but your actual total throughput or velocity along the whole process will be either unaffected or the improvements will be below their potential.

Value-stream mapping also provides an opportunity for communication, coordination, and buy-in along the whole value stream—prerequisites for a successful lean intervention.

WHAT IS A VALUE-STREAM MAP?

A value stream is the set of activities—both value-adding and non-value-adding—that makes up a business process. For example:

- In manufacturing, it consists of the activities involved in transforming raw material into product and bringing it to the customer.

- In the office, the value stream includes all processes and roles that create value, or are essential to creating value.

A value-stream map is a visual representation of the flow of materials and information through the value stream. It is a simple, concrete, "paper-and-pencil" tool that traces the current flow of value from end to end. This map then provides inputs for visualizing the future "ideal" and implementing lean to attain this state.

There are three tangible end products of a value-stream map exercise, described in the following sections.

A Current-State Map

A current-state map is a picture of what is. It's different from a typical process flow in that it is a picture of what is actually happening in the process. A process flow looks at the steps involved in the process, whereas the value-stream map goes much further than that. With the data on the map, you can determine all of the following:

- The health of your process

- Where the bottlenecks are

- How much work is in the system

- What people are doing

- How many are doing it right

- How the process actually works, which can be different from the way it was originally intended

It is important to recall that the purpose of the current-state map is to give you a basis on which to create a future-state map and a lean office implementation plan (described in the next two sections). The implications of this are simple: the *value-stream map does not need to be perfect*. It only has to be good enough to identify areas for improvement.

A Future-State Map

A future-state map envisions what your process will look like once you have effected improvements in all the areas identified. It should be aligned with the broader strategic objectives and vision. The future state is not necessarily etched in stone—once the lean implementation plan is put into action, you may notice that changes that were impossible at the time of current-state mapping have now become attainable. Measuring the impact of lean on a continuous basis and modifying the future state accordingly are essential for maximizing the success of lean.

The Lean Implementation Plan

The lean implementation plan is the most important document in the value-stream map process. This plan outlines what you will work on, in order to create the vision you captured in the future-state map.

Some value-stream workshops, for whatever reason, go slower than expected. If, after creating the current-state map, you are running out of time, skip the future-state map, and go straight to the lean implementation plan. Why? Lean is about action. *You can move immediately when you have an implementation plan*; you can't when you only have a future-state map.

WHY MAP THE VALUE STREAM?

A value-stream mapping exercise helps you understand the larger context of your processes, including systems, suppliers, and customers. This is the beauty of value-stream mapping. It highlights how each process impacts, and is impacted by, forces and elements outside its confines.

The value-stream map is rich in data, and it promotes decision making based on thorough data analysis. Although the data captured only represents a moment in time, it provides a sound basis for an effective implementation plan. Value-stream mapping helps you decide where to start, and it sets the direction for where you may go. Prioritizing issues, however, can be challenging. The value-stream map is a unique way to visualize data about your process, your organization, your suppliers, and your customers.

For many organizations, value-stream mapping also provides a unique opportunity for cross-functional collaboration and learning. Too often, organizations are siloed, with departments acting independently of each other. In the value-stream-mapping exercise, employees get an opportunity to work together and learn about each other's processes. Emerging out of the understanding that all the departments together form the whole, it also engenders a healthy respect for the work done by other departments. Moreover, the map provides a common language or medium, which can be used across all organizational levels for understanding and addressing issues in the business process.

WHO SHOULD BE ON THE VALUE-STREAM-MAPPING TEAM

A change is most effective when it is planned, implemented, and owned by those who will be impacted by it. Therefore, the value-stream-mapping team should represent all roles and processes that are part of the value stream.

At the same time, it is important to remember that numbers do matter. If the team has too many members, group management issues may surface. If you are mapping a process that requires a large group, plan to break it up into sub-teams, and make sure that you have enough facilitators to manage those sub-teams.

If you don't have enough people from all the different parts of the process participating in the value-stream-mapping exercise, you may end up with an inaccurate map. It may also affect buy-in of the map and its implementation plan. If it is not practical to form a truly representative team, try to limit the mapping to those processes represented by the team members. Another option is to include members who can represent multiple functions or processes.

While the value-stream map has implications at the strategic level, its impact percolates to the line level and often cuts across functional boundaries. Hence the mapping team should include executives, managers, and subject-matter experts. If you are mapping the value stream as a preparation for kaizen, ensure that the team has at least a few members who will be involved with the kaizen.

Executives on the Value-Stream-Mapping Team

In most organizational structures, executives are the vital link between strategy and action. They need to understand the big picture—strategic objectives and vision—and at the same time, be tuned in to the operational details. Executives are aware of the destination, as well as the steps leading up to it. They often possess strategic information, which they may use to guide the team toward organizational goals. Their unique awareness of strategic issues makes them powerful change agents. Thus, executives have a fundamental role in value-stream mapping. The mapping process (and, at a broader level, lean implementation) may be initiated by top-level management and coordinated by executives who are involved with the respective business processes.

In many organizations, the facilitators, especially internal facilitators, are reluctant to include managers or executives in the value-stream-mapping exercise. The reluctance may stem from these concerns:

- The executive or manager may dominate the discussions, overwhelming others lower in the hierarchy.

- Those lower in the hierarchy may be reluctant to speak honestly for fear of reprimand, or worse, from the executive or manager.

In some instances, and in some organizations, these are realistic concerns. On the other hand, sometimes managers will swing to the other extreme and hold back their views, for fear of dominating the discussions.

Here is where able facilitators can make all the difference. It is the facilitator's role to brief leaders on their roles and responsibilities, and make every participant—irrespective of hierarchy—comfortable and committed to contributing to the exercise. Although the executives must welcome the views and suggestions of those lower in the hierarchy, it is their responsibility to present their unique perspective on the processes in question in the context of the larger organization and business plan.

Why First-Level Managers Should Be on the Value-Stream-Mapping Team

First-level managers (FLMs) should be involved because they have an intimate understanding of how process works in the organization. From the change perspective, there are other important reasons to have FLMs involved, as described in the following paragraphs.

First-Level Managers May Be Affected by the Changes
Being on the team will give them a better chance to see how they fit into the changed scenario. To support the change process, FLMs need to see a future for themselves once the changes are made.

First-Level Managers Will Be Involved in Implementing the Changes
First-level managers hold the responsibility for running the show. Being a part of the team enables them to put things in perspective when implementation occurs (e.g., the reasons behind the changes, the context, and what exactly is to be done).

First-Level Managers Will Sustain the Changes
The FLMs hold the responsibility for ensuring that the changes are implemented in the way intended by the value-stream team. If the need for course corrections arises along the way, the FLMs will have a better understanding of possible impacts to the rest of the process.

First-Level Managers Will Measure and Report on Progress
First-level managers who participate on the team help determine how progress will be measured and reported. They can help select measures and reporting procedures that make sense, because they, ultimately, will use these measures.

Finally, including FLMs in the value-stream-mapping process expresses an organizational value—that of involving those who will be affected by a change in its design and implementation.

Why Subject Matter Experts (SMEs) Should Be on the Value-Stream-Mapping Team

The benefits of having the SMEs on the team include all those identified for the first-level managers in the previous section. There are also other unique benefits:

SMEs Know the Details of the Process

Their knowledge is usually thorough and up to date. They have the advantage of having seen the same application, perhaps used differently, in other firms or even industries. They bring a fresh perspective, often helping with firm benchmarking and out-of-the-box thinking. They can also point out bottlenecks and issues of which others (such as executives) may not be aware.

SMEs Know How the Process Works in Practice

They understand workarounds and temporary fixes. Their hands-on experience provides insights into the way things actually work, which is often different from the way they are supposed to work.

SMEs Can Help Mediate How the Changes Are Accepted

Because SMEs are often considered to be opinion leaders, both the executives and the FLMs find it easier to accept a stance or argument presented by SMEs. Once the SMEs own the change process, they can explain the rationale behind the changes and the expected results to their peers and the frontline staff with whom they work.

HOW TO MAP THE VALUE STREAM

Once you have decided to map your value stream, it is time to get the process rolling. Consulting a value-stream-mapping manual can give you a useful framework. Two books provide excellent information on value-stream mapping:

1. *The Complete Lean Enterprise* by Beau Keyte and Drew Locher[1]

2. *Value Stream Management for the Lean Office* by Don Tapping and Tom Shuker[2]

Both of them do an excellent job of illustrating how to value-stream map successfully. They include good descriptions of lean concepts that are important in the office environment and standard solutions for some common office processes.

NOTES

1. Beau Keyte, Drew Locher, *The Complete Lean Enterprise: Value Stream Mapping for Administrative and Office Processes* (New York: Productivity Press, 2004).

2. Don Tapping, Tom Shuker, *Value Stream Management for the Lean Office* (New York: Productivity Press, 2003).

CHAPTER 5

PREPARING FOR A KAIZEN IN THE OFFICE

Kaizen literally means "small, continuous improvements." Ensuring that your kaizen event brings about the desired improvements in a sustained manner involves a lot of groundwork, even when armed with a value-stream map (as discussed in Chapter 4) and an implementation plan.

In any intervention, adequate preparation is crucial for ensuring a successful outcome. This chapter discusses, in detail, the five preparatory activities that help enhance the success of your office kaizen event. Here's a quick overview:

1. Evaluating the situation

2. Developing a charter

3. Gathering data

4. Updating the charter

5. Planning for the kaizen

STEP 1: EVALUATING THE SITUATION

The first preparatory activity, and also the most difficult to define, is evaluating the situation. The objectives of this stage are:

- To validate readiness for an office kaizen

- To identify other preparatory activities, if required

- To get a sense of the information that will populate the kaizen charter

Evaluation depends heavily on the specific situation and the experience and judgment of the people involved. How do you know that an area is ready for an office kaizen? You never really know for sure, but there are several indicators. As a general guideline, the next sections describe factors to consider when conducting an evaluation.

Assess Your Sponsor's Support for the Kaizen

The first and most important factor in enabling readiness for a kaizen event is sponsorship. The sponsor must be available and willing to support the effort. If the identity of the sponsor is not clear, or the sponsor is uninvolved or distracted, it can adversely impact the kaizen endeavor. If the sponsor is unsupportive but wants to proceed with the event, you may need to unravel his or her true motivation and link it with your efforts to garner the sponsor's involvement and support.

Don't Worry Yet About Documenting Processes

Some lean consultants believe that the organization should have its processes documented before proceeding with a lean event. Although several arguments favor this stance, current documentation is not essential. In fact, attempting to document the existing processes in the way it is traditionally done—in a conference room or some place removed from where the work is conducted—may waste time. Often, documented processes do not represent what actually happens. This occurs when organizations document their processes without using lean tools and principles. Later sections in this chapter detail how to accurately document processes.

Make Sure Managers Are Involved in the Project

Another area that could come under the spotlight during evaluation is the level of involvement of the managers. It is a positive sign when managers are onboard for processes targeted for office kaizen and engaged with the idea of a lean office. If managers show resistance or opposition to the idea, it may help to probe further about what they really think and feel. If they are doubtful or disinterested, invite them to approach the effort as an experiment. If managers can merely open their mind to the possibility of learning something, then this outlook demonstrates another positive step. Questioning the validity of lean (or the validity of anything else, for that matter) signals that the questioner is thinking, and that he or she cares. Everyone has different experiences and different viewpoints, which need to be valued and encouraged

Figure 5–1 is a list of questions that you may use for understanding a business process, and for assessing the readiness of the organization to undertake an office kaizen.

STEP 2: DEVELOPING A CHARTER

The charter is among the most important documents in a successful office kaizen event. Serving as a blueprint for the event, it forces you to think critically about what you want, how you want to do it, and what success will look

---

Questions to ask about work processes before undertaking an office kaizen

1. Is this project part of a lean implementation plan developed in a value-stream-map exercise?
2. What are the criteria for evaluation?
3. Who owns the process?
4. Is the sponsor involved?
5. Are processes documented?
6. Do the documented processes bear any resemblance to what actually happens?
7. What is the level of employee morale?
8. Is the work area or electronic workspace well organized?
9. What are the metrics?
10. How are the metrics used?
11. How often are metrics recorded?
12. Are there metrics that tell employees how they are doing at any point in time?
13. What is the attitude toward customers? Are the employees customer focused, or are they unaware of or disrespectful toward the customer?
14. What is the attitude toward change?
15. What are the business goals and strategies, and is the proposed project aligned with them?
16. Is the process repeatable?
17. Who is involved in the process?
18. Whom does the process impact?
19. Who inputs or supplies the process?
20. Who is the receiver or the customer of the process?

Figure 5-1.

like. This may seem like a lot of paperwork with no action, but resist the temptation to adopt shortcuts in this part of the process. A clear and succinct charter increases the likelihood that the goals will be reached and ensures that the office kaizen team knows exactly what to do. Moreover, a well-planned charter will eventually allow you and the kaizen team to determine whether the goal has been achieved.

The charter acts as a guideline for team members to use whenever they get stuck. It forms a basis for analyzing how the team is working, and in what context the team is operating. Sometimes, organizations lack the patience to spend sufficient time on a charter. Admittedly, documentation does not sound half as exciting as actually "doing." However, a little planning now will reduce confusion and rework later. With this in mind, categorize the elements of the charter as *project elements* and *team elements*. These elements are described in detail in later sections. Figure 5–2 shows a sample office kaizen chart that illustrates one company's elements.

Defining the Kaizen Project Elements

The kaizen charter should include six key project elements, which answer the following questions:

1. What is this event about? (**subject**)

2. What are the contextual factors that impact the subject? (**background**)

3. What specific improvement do you want to achieve? (**targets**)

4. What are the specific limits of the kaizen event? (**boundaries**)

5. What are the specific start and end dates for each of the three phases of the kaizen event? (**timeline**)

6. Within the boundaries, how big and complex is the process, and how much work will it take to achieve the targets? (**scope**)

The following sections describe each of these elements in more detail.

Subject
The subject of the event answers the question, "What is the event about?" Here are some examples of subjects:

• Create a continuous flow production schedule process.

• Improve customer-service response time and customer-satisfaction scores.

• Develop a standard process for purchasing supplies.

• Improve the way performance metrics are reported.

Subject	Create a continuous flow production schedule process	Sponsor: Jane Doe
Background	<ul><li>The existing production scheduling process involves three departments: engineering, sales, and production.</li><li>Customer service scores have declined since the merger and relocation 9 months ago. Two new products have been introduced, one of which has had production quality problems. We have not received support information for the new products.</li><li>It currently takes three weeks to collect and report performance metrics. Leadership wants more current inforamtion with which to make decisions.</li></ul>	
Targets	<ul><li>Reduce the cycle time of order entry process from 9 minutes to 5 minutes</li><li>Balance workload to pitch of 10 orders per hour</li></ul>	
Boundaries	Includes: • Order entry • Credit and accounting • Purchasing • Outside sales	Excludes: • Engineering • Manufacturing
Timeline	Preparation: August 10 – September 25 Office kaizen: September 27 – September 29 1-2-3 reports: October 29, November 27, and January 5	
Team members	Team leader: Prem Kumar Team members: • Benjamin Ng • Armando Lopez • Jerry Oakman • Shin Siev • Irma Nyseth • Carol Tibbets	

Figure 5-2. Office kaizen charter

Once again, make sure that the subject is aligned with the business goal. Ultimately, it's not about process improvement—it's about *business success.*

When constructing the subject, keep it short. This helps the team and other stakeholders clearly define the project goals.

Background

The background section of the charter answers the question, "What are the contextual factors that impact the subject?" It helps to communicate the relevance of the project by highlighting the pertinent details surrounding the project. Here are some examples:

- "The existing production scheduling process involves three departments: engineering, sales, and production."

- "Customer service scores have declined since the merger and relocation 9 months ago. Two new products have been introduced; one of which has had production quality problems. We have not received support information for the new products."

- "The manager currently buys supplies for the area and wishes to delegate that process to her direct reports. However, there are no standard processes or min/max triggers for ordering supplies."

- "It currently takes 3 weeks to collect and report performance metrics. Leadership wants more current information with which to make decisions."

The background helps communicate the relevance of the project and forces the team to think about the context.

Targets

You need a clear bull's eye to know where to aim. Targets must be tangible, observable, specific, and measurable. Targets cannot be an opinion or judgment. You must be able to measure them on a scale or in binary form (for instance, with a "yes" or "no" answer to questions about meeting the target) and also verify them. They must be relevant to leadership, management, employees, and/or customers.

Here are some formats and examples of specific targets:

- Format: [direction of change] the [type of measure] of [name of process or procedure] from x to y.

- Example: "Reduce the cycle time of order entry process from 9 minutes to 5 minutes."

Boundaries

Boundaries mark the limits of the event. There are many ways of defining boundaries, such as "includes x and excludes y," or "from this part of the process to that part of the process," or something similar. Here are sample boundary statements from actual office kaizens:

- "The service order process from its arrival on the scheduler's desk, through production processes to final billing. Excludes actual production, product finishing, and product shipping operations."

- "Employee on-boarding process, from receipt of acceptance letter to employee's first day. Excludes executive and international hires."

Boundaries also help the team members stay clear about their goals. Without the clarity that boundaries bring, teams tend to have a difficult time focusing on the task at hand. Boundaries tell the team—and individuals within the team—what to work on and what to ignore.

Boundaries help prevent "mission creep." In the excitement of the event, or even when planning the event, there can be pressure to increase the scope of the event. Often, even without intent, the scope gets elastic and stretches beyond the original plan. Sometimes, there is a reasonable explanation for this, but more often than not, it does not make sense. Teams need to stay within the boundaries defined in the charter. Many teams are interested in productive work, and that can translate into "more" work. And more work is not necessarily the right work to do. Boundaries help the team stay focused on the right work—the work defined by the planning team or the value-stream-map implementation plan.

Sometimes, it becomes clear that something outside the boundaries has to be addressed or included in order for progress to occur. It's acceptable to *change* the boundaries, but *be clear about why you are doing it*. Ascertain whether changing the boundaries requires adjustments in team size, team composition, or the timetable for the event.

Timeline

The timeline contains three key timeframes:

- The preparation

- The kaizen event

- The follow-up reports

For the purposes of the charter, each phase should have a single bar with start and end dates—like a Gantt chart. The idea is to provide a high-level idea of the schedule.

Phase 1: Preparing for the kaizen. The preparation phase is the most important phase of the office kaizen. It includes all the tasks that create inputs required for a successful office kaizen. In fact, you can consider the preparation phase as part of the kaizen. Most people think that the kaizen is where all the magic happens. Well, in a real magic show, the magician presents crowd-pleasing tricks because he has spent an enormous amount of time—sometimes a lifetime—on preparation. The same holds true for the kaizen event. *A successful kaizen depends on successful preparation.* In a large organization, a 5-day office kaizen requires 4 to 6 weeks of preparation.

That said, it is possible to have a successful kaizen without formal preparation. An organization that is familiar and experienced with kaizen events is, in fact, always prepared because the people have been trained in lean principles and are currently practicing them at work.

Phase 2: Conducting the kaizen. The kaizen varies in length, depending on the following factors:

- The complexity of the organization

- The organization's goals

- The size of the team

- The boundaries

Larger organizations with complex, interlocking processes can afford to spare a team for 5 days. Smaller organizations can have shorter kaizens.

The shortest office kaizen this author has run, lasted about 4 hours. Of course, there was a lot of preparation and follow-up work, but at least the employees were not taken away from their work for an extended period of time. What was sacrificed was the training of employees in lean principles, as well as limiting the scope of impact. In this particular case, the team was facilitated through some process development work without using lean terminology that would have otherwise required additional training. The business owner was taught some basic lean concepts, again without the technical terminology.

Terminology has three potential problems:

1. It can be off-putting.

2. It can slow down progress.

3. It can be non-value-adding.

Terminology works best for lean practitioners, who are able to communicate complicated concepts and bundled ideas with a single word. In dealing with nonexperts, however, sometimes it is just as easy to tell them what they have to do, without attaching a Japanese or otherwise technical term. Of course, there is a downside to using "plain language." It can make communicating with other professionals more difficult, but that is irrelevant in the big picture.

Phase 3: Reporting on the kaizen after completion. The post-kaizen stage ultimately determines whether the preparation and the kaizen event were successful. People tend to like the feeling of accomplishment that they experience in the office kaizen event. The more mundane day-to-day work is less satisfying and exciting, but this is where the real payoff is achieved.

Follow-through topics are covered in chapters 6 and 7. But it is important to capture the follow-on activities up front, so that it is understood that it is part of the whole picture, and without it, the whole event is incomplete.

In fact, kaizen should be perceived as a *project* rather than as a *one-time event*. When kaizen is defined as an event, it short-changes or diminishes the importance of preparation and follow-up/sustaining activities. The office kaizen is the party phase. The event becomes a waste, unless it is preceded by thorough preparation and followed by adequate effort to sustain the improvements.

Scope

The scope of the office kaizen refers to the size of the process within the boundaries, combined with the targets. In short, it is the amount of work to be done on that process in the kaizen event. Focus on projects that are important enough to devote the attention that the office kaizen requires, or scale them down so that you can devote the attention it requires to be successful.

Assembling the Kaizen Team

There are distinct roles for the kaizen team:

- The sponsor (who is not really a member of the team but who must support the team's work)

- The team leader

- A lean leader or facilitator

- A project manager

- Team members (fulltime)

- Team members (on-call)

The role of each is described in the following sections.

Sponsor

Who is a sponsor? A sponsor is the individual who has budget authority over the process being changed. The sponsor also has the authority to hire and dismiss those who administer the process in question.

What does the sponsor do? The sponsor has several key responsibilities, including:

- Sanctioning the office kaizen. By authorizing the event, the sponsor conveys the importance of the event to everyone in the organization, and that the kaizen has his or her full support.

- Approving the goals set for the office kaizen. The sponsor confirms that the goals put forth in the charter are consistent and aligned with the organization's business strategy and goals.

- Providing the resources required to complete the office kaizen successfully.

- Authorizing the right personnel to be part of the team.

- Tracking and supporting the changes produced by the office kaizen:

  - Removing any obstacles in the way of a successful office kaizen.

  - Attending the team kick-off and report-out.

The Kaizen Team

Any project is only as productive as the people who run it. Even the most ingenious plan acquires value only when it is implemented by the right set of people. The team that runs a kaizen event should comprise representatives from each part of the process. But it is not necessary that every kaizen team member be involved with the process, or even that they know the process. In fact, for training purposes, people unconnected to the process may be included. These people, when engaged in the kaizen team, often bring a fresh perspective that the others may not have. These "outsiders" can bring value to the team and improve the quality of the output. The team may also have subject experts, but this is not essential. The members who are part of the process just need to know how to do their jobs, and be able to explain their jobs to others on the team.

In addition to the functions represented by the team members, pay attention to the temperamental composition of the team. Apart from representing different sets of knowledge, job functions, and experience, the kaizen team should ideally include people with diverse attitudes and competencies. For instance, every team should include opinion leaders who can influence their peers and facilitate the acceptance of change. Often, the opinion leaders are people who set standards for others by virtue of their expertise or experience. You also need to have some members who will question and challenge the views and decisions of the majority. An exclusive bunch of "yes-people" seldom creates anything new or valuable. You need people who are not afraid to stray from the herd—often, these team members force the team to think through difficult and sensitive issues and devise productive solutions.

Once you have chosen the team members, you can slot them into the appropriate roles, as previously listed and further described in the following sections.

The Team Leader

The team leader owns primary responsibility for the outcome of the kaizen. He or she makes sure that the team has the resources it needs, and that obstacles are identified and addressed. The team leader attends to the needs of the team, ensuring that they stay on track—within the boundaries—and remain focused on the goals.

The Lean Leader or Facilitator

This person makes sure the team understands the lean improvement process and follows it before, during, and after the office kaizen. The lean facilitator coaches the team members on how to apply the lean concepts in their particular situation, and also helps the team leader keep the team moving.

The lean facilitator plays a support role, in the sense that he or she does not own the process being worked on, or its outcomes. The lean facilitator is an advocate of the broader lean process and is responsible for the overall lean outcomes. He or she may coach the team on the lean tools and techniques and how to apply them, but the ultimate responsibility for the team outcomes rests with the team leader and the sponsor.

Project Manager

The project manager helps the team leader keep track of the schedule and is often responsible for assigning specific tasks to individuals or subteams. The project manager assists with resource allocation and removal of obstacles—especially at the "hands-on" level. The project manager may also help supervise team members and support them to ensure optimum performance. In smaller teams or events, the team leader may also function as the project manager.

Team Members

The team members are responsible for bringing to the fore their experience, talent, and wisdom in working toward the team goals. Each team member works on his or her part of the project, and the members help each other understand the process in its entirety. Apart from the full-time members, "guest members" may be called in to work on specific parts of the process or offer solutions to a particular problem. The team members generate, select, design, test, and implement solutions to achieve the goals set forth in the charter.

Delegating Decision Making for the Kaizen Project

Decision making is an issue closely related to the involvement theme. In every team, the authority to make decisions is delegated. In the case of the office kaizen, the sponsor delegates decision making to the team. By agreeing to sanction the event, the sponsor is, in effect, saying to the team, "I entrust you with the responsibility to make the necessary decisions required to achieve the goals in the charter, within the boundaries stated in the charter." This, by the way, is why the charter is so important, and also why the sponsor's buy-in and clarity around the charter are essential.

The charter is a guiding document that helps delegate decision making. The charter makes sure that the right information is being transferred so that the team can see success. Sponsors can be coached to accept what the team devises and to allow the team to implement it. The charter gives them the confidence to reach this level of delegation.

In situations where sponsors are uncomfortable delegating on the basis of a charter, request progress reports from the team during the course of the kaizen. This enables them to track progress, and it provides both corrective input and encouragement. If this is done—and it does not need to be done constantly, nor does it need to take an inordinate amount of time—the sponsor can be more confident about the outcome.

Another ground rule for team improvements is that they should cost little money. The team should be encouraged to work with what it has at its disposal. There might be minor expenditures, but large expenses should be avoided. If, for some reason, the team does come up with a costly proposal, suggest that they put that idea into the action item list and do the business case for it *outside* the context of the office kaizen. Fancy, expensive solutions often do not focus on reducing waste—the very thing that is draining profit from the organization.

Accepting expensive solutions also allows the team to avoid using their natural creativity for devising real, cost-effective ways to achieve the project targets. The power of office kaizen is that *it can yield real-world solutions that can be implemented immediately.* There is no reason to wait for someone else to solve the team's problems with a system or packaged solution.

Sponsors need to accept the output of the team, regardless of what it is (unless, of course, the implementation would prove obviously catastrophic). After all the work the team puts into generating a solution, being told that its plan needs prior approval before implementation, or that the sponsor does not like the idea will demotivate the team and delay the process. Generally, if the sponsor dislikes or does not understand the team's solution, it is because the sponsor has not kept track of the team's progress and/or has not been clear about the charter elements. However hard it may be for sponsors to accept, the fact is that they are directly responsible for the successful outcome of the team. The only way to circumvent an unfortunate turn of events is to prepare the sponsor and make him or her aware of what his or her role entails and ensure the sponsor's commitment to the task ahead.

Differentiating Management Decisions and Team Decisions

Empowering the kaizen team with decision-making authority speeds up the event, boosts the morale of team members, and encourages them to achieve the targets. Sometimes, however, management may need to step in to decide on certain matters, particularly those with strategic, long-term, or organizational-level implications.

Therefore, it is important for team members to know the scope and limits of their authority. They need to know when to make decisions on their own and when to defer the decision to management. Being open about decision making and documenting how decisions will be made can go a long way toward bringing about clarity.

STEP 3: GATHERING DATA

Once the charter is complete, data gathering can begin. The charter will help the data-gathering process stay focused on the kaizen objectives.

Select Data Gatherers

Those workers who actually do the work should gather the data. In other words, people should gather data on their own jobs. There are several benefits to this:

- There is greater acceptance of the data.

- The employees get a fresh look at how they do their work, and they get a chance to see and recognize issues firsthand.

- They can develop possible solutions even as they collect the data.

Let's look at each benefit in more detail.

Greater Acceptance of the Data

There will be greater acceptance of the data if the applicable workers collect it themselves. There is a natural tendency to distrust data on their work when someone else collects it. This tendency is even more pronounced when an expert who is perceived to be an "outsider" collects it. When employees collect data on their own work, they have an opportunity to view it from a fresh perspective. Often, work is done with varying levels of automaticity—that is, people, especially experienced employees, automatically know what to do without examining every move.

A Fresh, Firsthand Perspective on How They Work

While collecting data, workers also gain a new perspective on many issues. When they observe issues firsthand, they are more accepting of what they see. In contrast, when someone else points out issues, a natural dynamic emerges in the form of resistance, whereas when they, personally, collect the data, they are confronted with what they see. If they deny what they see—well, that is a different issue and requires a different kind of intervention than those provided by lean tools.

An Opportunity to Develop Solutions

Recognizing issues during data collection gives the data-gatherers an opportunity to develop possible solutions before the office kaizen workshop actually starts. Ideas developed before the start of the workshop can be considered along with those generated during the workshop itself.

Go to Where the Work Is Done

"Go to the gemba" is a common refrain in lean manufacturing. It means "go to where the work is done." It makes sense, and that approach may be used in the office environment, too.

The biggest mistake a team can make is to use existing documentation as a proxy for *what actually happens* in the office. Existing documentation rarely matches the reality of what happens in a process—here are just a few reasons why:

- Documentation does not indicate waiting, watching, or wandering.

- Documentation does not capture interruptions, incomplete work, or many other intangibles.

- Documentation rarely captures the actual step-by-step processes that happen in the real world, with the accuracy and detail required by the kaizen team.

- Another problem with relying on existing documentation is that it deprives the team of the learning opportunities afforded by real-time observation.

Another mistake similar to using existing documentation is relying on *personal accounts* and *memories* of what a job entails. Although memory may be sufficient for value-stream mapping, memories are often inaccurate, and thus insufficient, for kaizen. What employees *remember* about their work and what they *actually do* are two different things. This does not mean that the employees are lying. Often, it simply implies that they are so good at what they do that they do many tasks automatically. People are great judges of their own experiences, but judgment is often swayed by our attention. When team members take the time to observe their colleagues doing the work that they know so well, these team members see what they forgot or treat as part of the scenery: those things that have become routine or second nature.

"Going to where the work is done" in the office environment is a little more complicated than "going to the gemba" in a factory or shop environment. The reason is that many processes in the office cannot be readily observed like a factory process. Office processes may leap from a thought process, to a computer process, to a conversation, to a decision process, and so forth.

In the next section, "Map the Process Flows," you will learn how to capture and document what you see in the office. You will even learn how to capture and document what you don't see in the office: data and thinking.

Mapping the Process Flows

Mapping process flows—both visible and invisible—poses an interesting challenge in the office environment. Documenting the flows gives you a snapshot in time of the current condition. It is not feasible, or even necessary, to capture every single condition, process uniqueness, or variation. You need to pick a typical product, order, etc. (or a few of them) to flow through your system as you capture the information. An important concept in process design and its improvement is to design solutions for the majority of your work. If you design solutions for your exceptions, you may end up with more cumbersome processes. With regard to the exceptions, seek to understand what causes them. Do a five-why root-cause analysis, and try to resolve the variation without adding wasteful workarounds.

Documenting your processes as described in the next section deepens your understanding of the process. *Documenting is not a passive process.* In fact, this is where the learning and change begin. The intense observation involved in process mapping makes it one of the most important, though underrated, activities in process improvement.

Documenting is a good starting point for identifying waste. As previously mentioned, many activities on the job are learned and unconscious. As long as immediate targets are being achieved, people rarely pause to analyze what they are doing—or how they are doing it. Putting the process in black and white gives people the opportunity to get an unbiased, as-is picture of the process. This makes it easier for them to detect where the waste is and how the flow of value is interrupted or reduced.

How to Map Flow

The purpose of mapping office flows is to understand how data is processed and transformed, and specifically how decisions, information, products, and services are made. Mapping the flows helps overcome the challenge that many have faced in applying lean principles in the office: making the fluid and sometimes invisible office flows visible. Once you have made the flows visible, you can more easily see where waste lives in your processes, and then make decisions about what to do about it.

To understand the flows within the office, it makes sense to return to the definition and purpose of the office: to process and transform data. This processing and transformation yields decisions, information, products, and services.

Decision making is a universal office activity practiced by office workers and management at every level. Mapping data that flow into decision points can help increase the quality of the decisions.

Information can be defined as the useful combination of data. Offices create a lot of information, and not all of it is useful. Process mapping helps clarify what information is really relevant, and what is not. A report that is not read exemplifies this type of useless information. (Imagine what the business world would be like if it were able to reduce unread reports by 50%!) At any rate, process mapping helps determine how the report is used. By analyzing how it is used, you will understand what components the user really values, and whether or not it is used at all.

Some offices create products and provide services as a core business activity. For them, mapping the processes constitutes the first step in creating a competitive advantage.

The key process flows covered here are people flow and data flow.

Mapping People Flow

People flow refers to the movement of people in space. In some cases, people don't move at all, and that will be noted. In other cases, they move a lot. When there is people flow, use a "spaghetti chart" to document that movement. On an 8.5" x 11" (or A4) sheet of paper, draw a rough layout of your office. Track the movement of people within that layout with lines following the path of movement. After a while, the chart begins to look like a plate of spaghetti (hence the name of the chart). Figure 5-3 is an example.

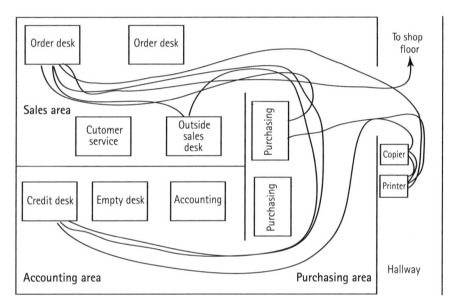

Figure 5-3. Spaghetti chart showing people flow

Using the spaghetti chart is simple:

1. Draw a rough outline of the work area being studied on the chart.

2. Then follow the movements of the worker as he or she performs the process that is under study.

3. As you follow the movements of the person, trace your pencil over the corresponding route on the spaghetti chart.

4. Once you have completed the observation using the spaghetti chart, estimate the distance traveled.

Another tool used to track people flow is the "standard work combination chart": Figure 5-4 is an example. This is a chart that captures three types of activities an office worker engages in—manual work, walking, and waiting.

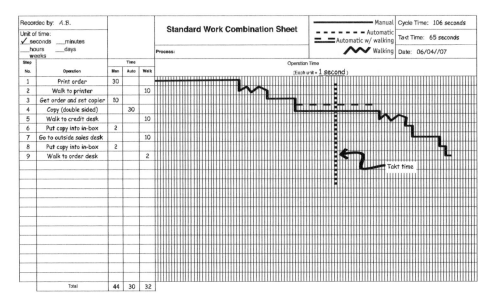

Figure 5-4. Standard work combination sheet

It also captures interruptions. Interruptions may be unavoidable in some cases, but they do consume much time. With every interruption comes a mental setup time to reengage with the work.

How to Capture Workload Balance

Balancing the work means distributing the work evenly along the process. This is achieved by managing capacity so that it is spread evenly among those engaged in the process. This not only involves efficient *allocation of work*, but it also demands better flow among the different sets of employees or departments to avoid bottlenecks—pockets of time when everyone seems to be waiting for someone else to finish. This presupposes a clear understanding of the workflow and its sequence, along with estimated and realistic timelines.

To illustrate this idea, reconsider the scenario introduced in Chapter 3 in the section entitled "Method #9: Workload Leveling." In that scenario, a large mail-order pharmacy has an order-entry process that begins with these two steps: enter order, and then verify eligibility. In this case, the rate of customer demand, or takt time, is one order per minute. On average, the time to enter an order takes 45 seconds. The average time to verify eligibility is 1 minute and 15 seconds. The workload is unbalanced because the time to process a claim is unequal between entry and verification. The challenge here is to find a way to balance the workload so that each step takes 1 minute—equal to the rate of customer demand.

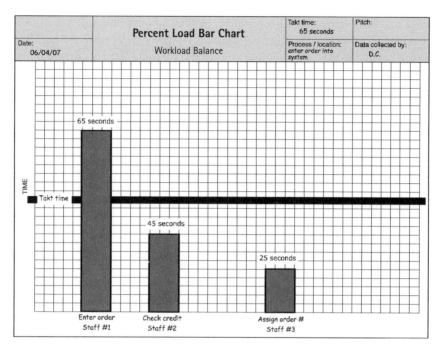

Figure 5-5. Percent load bar chart

Refer to Figure 5-5 to see how to chart this scenario.

There are two obvious possibilities. The first is to see if there is some way to shift 15 seconds of task load from verification to entry. The second is to eliminate 15 seconds of process waste from the verification process.

How to Determine Process [or Work-System] Capacity

The slowest process in the system determines the process capacity (just like the old saying, "a chain is only as strong as its weakest link"). So if you can calculate how much work is involved in that process, you can determine the process capacity. If the process capacity falls below the rate of customer demand, then you have a target. If it is above the rate of customer demand, then you have excess capacity that you might allocate to other areas.

If the process capacity falls below the rate of customer demand, it does not make sense to improve the process elsewhere, because the flow will just be constricted by the bottleneck. Also, it makes no sense to have other parts of the process create at a rate greater than the bottleneck. The process capacity needs to be improved before moving on to other areas. Fixing every problem "then and there" is in fact the true essence of kaizen.

Referring to the previously mentioned, pharmacy mail-order process example, order entry time is 45 seconds, and the verification process takes 1 minute and 15 seconds. Because the verification process is the slower one, the total process capacity for those two steps is one order every one minute and 15 seconds.

STEP 4: UPDATING THE CHARTER

The data you have collected and the process of collection give you new insights into the process. You can now review the charter in light of this new learning, by asking the following questions.

Is the Subject the Right One?

The subject *per se* rarely changes, but sometimes team leaders learn something new that suggests a modification, if not a change, in the subject. This does not happen often, but you should be aware of the possibility.

For example, a manager from the IT department of a global electronics manufacturer decided to form a kaizen to improve an internal computing hardware storage and reissue process. At the outset, he wanted to accomplish two goals:

1. Reduce the amount of space required to store the equipment

2. Reduce the lead time to respond to customer requests

The client wanted to complete the project before an employee laptop upgrade 3 months from the planned kaizen date. In isolation, these constitute positive process goals.

However, it was discovered that the motivation for the changes were more complicated than they appeared on the surface. A senior director over the project had other concerns. He believed too many people were going to claim the need for a new laptop when the upgrade was scheduled. He hoped that improving his process would reduce the need for new laptops. Again, this constitutes a good goal. The question was, would improving his process really change the behavior of employees who wanted brand-new laptops?

He had other concerns as well. The repair supply chain was "too slow." Inventory records were inaccurate. Processes varied at different storage locations.

With all these concerns, It was recommended that the client not do this kaizen at all. It made more sense for his group to value-stream map his process, and then make process improvement decisions based on data reflecting the entire process. The issue about employees requesting laptops they did not need was not his issue to control. That responsibility belonged to each employee's manager.

Are the Targets the Right Ones?

After studying the process, validate that the targets on the charter are the right ones. It is common to make adjustments to the targets. The type of target may remain the same, but the numbers might change. For example, a client from a printing company needed help. Printing is a competitive business, and the client wanted to position the printing company as the "rapid response" printing company. He had a target of simplifying a work-scheduling process for printing orders. Data needed to be collected on the process before specifying or quantifying the improvement.

Once data was compiled, he set the target. In this case, he set a target of decreasing the cycle time from 48 hours to 24 hours. Improvements of 50% are reasonable targets when using lean methods. In fact, *the team was able to reduce the cycle time by 93%*. He was surprised by that dramatic increase, but it was made possible because both the people who do the work, as well as the customer, were on the team.

How did the customer make a difference? It was discovered that the customer provided paperwork in the package that he thought the company needed, and that paperwork was processed thinking that the customer needed it. In fact, that particular part of the process was really not needed by anyone. Clearing this miscommunication between the customer and the client simplified the process.

Safety and ergonomic targets identified in the data collection need to be put on the charter. Healthy employees are productive employees. Also, attending to safety issues sends a strong message that management cares about its employees. This message supports good morale.

Are the Boundaries and Scope Appropriate?

The data or changes in the target may call for changes in the boundaries and scope of the kaizen event. You may need to adjust the boundaries of the event to include new areas, or exclude areas you previously thought made sense.

When you need to change the boundaries, determine how the scope of the event is affected. Was more work created, or was the amount of work originally required reduced? Do you have the right number of people on the team to get the work done? Make sure that corresponding adjustments are made in resource allocation, team size, and event schedule.

Do You Have the Right Team Members?

Take a solid look at the goals, and ask yourself: Do I have the right people on the team to achieve these targets? The answer does not always lie in the number of people. The important points are:

- The people who work on the processes are represented on the team.

- You have the right support and expertise on the team.

The people who work the process on a daily basis are the experts, and their involvement will increase the likelihood of their compliance.

Having the right support on the team is also important. For example, teams are often improving processes involving office automation—computing, software, and the like. Those who work the computers may not understand programming or systems, so an expert is included in those areas. For example, one team included a web developer, because the process had a customer interface on the company intranet.

STEP 5: PLAN THE AGENDA FOR THE OFFICE KAIZEN WORKSHOP

The last step in preparing for the kaizen event is to develop a step-by-step agenda. While deciding on the activities, remember that the challenge is in managing the team for success, and providing the right kind of training for the team to succeed. The overall structure of a kaizen workshop is simple:

1. Kick-off

2. Just-in-time training

3. Process walk

4. Identifying waste and other process issues

5. Simulating possible solutions (try-storming)

6. Selecting the solutions

7. Implementing the solutions

The details of this agenda, as well as how to conduct a kaizen in the office, are covered in Chapter 6.

CHAPTER 6

CONDUCTING A KAIZEN IN THE OFFICE

With the preparation in place, you are now ready to have a kaizen in the office. From the beginning kickoff to the final report-out, kaizen workshops can be exciting and productive for everyone involved. No matter what the final outcome, it is a valuable learning experience and an opportunity for team development.

THE KICKOFF

One of the powerful qualities of the way lean is practiced is standardization. That quality is expressed from the beginning of the office kaizen workshop by using a standard agenda. The formal kickoff, which should last no longer than 20 minutes, should include the agenda items shown in Figure 6-1. The sections that follow Figure 6–1 explain why each item on the agenda is important.

---

1. Introductions
2. Charter
3. Summary of data collection
4. Message from sponsor
5. Message from team leader
6. Message from lean coach/consultant
7. Questions for clarification

Figure 6-1. Sample agenda for an office kaizen

Introduce the Kaizen Team

The lean leader facilitates the kickoff. He leads by reviewing the kickoff agenda, and then starts the introductions. Introductions are important when individuals present are unfamiliar with one another. Introductions should be limited, for example, to name, organization, and job title. When those are complete, the lean leader turns the meeting over to the team leader.

Review the Kaizen Charter

The team leader begins by quickly reviewing the charter, team list, and daily target sheet. Even though the daily target sheet is a copy of the targets from the charter, it is shown so everyone understands that progress against the targets will be tracked on a daily basis.

Summarize the Data Already Collected

The team leader then shows and summarizes the data collected. This should be kept at a high level, giving broad-stroke information. The purpose of this is to give everyone an idea of what the data tell you at this point. The team will have time to explore the information in more detail later.

Get Support from the Sponsor

The message from the sponsor is a critical part of the kickoff. The sponsor should put the workshop in context, explaining the larger implications of the goals. He or she should also explain why the workshop is important. He or she should express support to the team, and offer to help with obstacles the team cannot handle.

Introduce the Team Leader and Lean Leader's Message

The message from the team leader should express, from his or her perspective, why the workshop is important. The message from the lean leader should tie the other two messages together, if necessary.

Allow Time for Questions from the Team

The kickoff ends with questions and clarifications. The purpose of this part is to answer questions to further the understanding of what was presented. Some may use this as an opportunity to further their agenda, propose solutions, be negative, etc. They should be reminded that this is not the right time to explore those issues. The intent of this section is to further the understanding of the team so that they achieve success.

JUST-IN-TIME TRAINING

Just-in-time training covers basic lean concepts and knowledge required to understand and work effectively within the office kaizen workshop process.

The typical training includes the following:

- Lean concept overview

- Types of waste

- Lean tools: visual process chart, standard work-combination sheet, 5-why process, spaghetti chart, simulation tools, decision-making tools, action item list, stakeholder analysis, and so on.

Provide an Overview of Lean Concepts

The lean concept overview is a quick introduction or review of the lean concepts covered in Chapter 3. The depth and speed with which you cover this and other topics depend on the previous lean experience of the team. Even with an experienced team, the highlights of the lean principles often need to be reviewed in relation to the workshop at hand.

Review the Common Types of Waste and Find Waste in Your Office

Reviewing the concept of waste and the types of waste that occur in an office environment is always a beneficial exercise. After reviewing the types of waste with the group, give everyone a list of the types of waste on a single sheet of paper (see Figure 6–2). Then ask them to go in groups of two to the work environment on a "waste walk" during which they look for wastes. This is a useful, practical way to get people to not just think about waste, but also develop an "eye" for it. Ask them to return in 15 to 30 minutes and share with the team what they saw. Not only does this exercise serve as training, it serves as a practical diagnostic tool that may prove useful during the workshop. This also helps them actually "see" what they need to set right, and start thinking in that direction.

Discuss Tools to Eliminate Office Waste

After the waste walk, review the standard lean tools that will be used in the workshop. You don't need to share every tool in the beginning. There is no point in teaching about tools not used during the workshop. If a need arises for a tool that has not been introduced, provide an impromptu "just-in-time" training for either the whole team or the subteam that will be using that tool.

Information Waste	Process Waste
1. Redundant input and output of data	1. Defects
2. Incompatible information systems	2. Scrap
3. Manual checking of data that has been entered electronically	3. Rework
4. Data dead-ends (i.e., data that is input but never used)	4. Workarounds
5. Reentering data	5. Inspecting, checking, and double-checking
6. Converting formats	6. Need for approvals
7. Unnecessary data	7. Variable flow in a process
8. Unavailable, unknown, or missing data	8. Too much inventory
9. Incorrect data	9. Incomplete work
10. Data safety issues (i.e., lost or incorrect data)	10. Overproduction
11. Unclear or incorrect data definitions	11. Waiting
12. Data discrepancies	12. Overprocessing
Physical environment waste	**Types of People Waste**
1. Safety	1. Unclear role (responsibility, authority, and accountability)
2. Movement	2. Lack of training
	3. Work or task interruptions
	4. Multitasking
	5. Underutilization of talent
	6. Recruitment errors
	7. Lack of strategic focus

Figure 6-2. Types of waste

It is important to teach concepts and tools, not solutions, to the team. *Generating solutions is the team's job.* If you (instead of the team) propose solutions, two things may happen. One, you may discourage the team's own generative creativity by "filling in the blank" with your own ideas. This could prevent them from devising better ideas. After all, they are the experts in the processes that they are working on in the workshop.

Second, you could unintentionally create resistance to what might actually be a useful idea. For whatever reason, people are more amenable to their own ideas. Chances are that if you think of a way to improve the process, someone else will think of it, too. If not, you may tactfully float your idea later in the workshop, but not during the training.

BUILD A WORKFLOW CHART

Building a workflow chart is a key exercise in understanding the office or service process. This tool will help the team make the whole process visible in one place. Without this step, comprehensive solutions are more difficult to develop.

To make this process-flow chart effective, the team needs to pick a typical scenario to run through the process. Some teams find this difficult because they perceive many distinctions in the work they do. The team has to start somewhere, however, so they need to pick a scenario that represents the largest or most important category of work that goes through that particular process.

A practical idea is to use a long stretch of white paper that comes in rolls. The chart may be several feet long and 3 or 4 feet high. Running the length of the paper, demarcate two lanes:

1. The process-as-observed lane

2. The process-solutions lane.

Here is how to use them.

In the *process-as-observed* lane, the team uses square or rectangular sticky notes to document the steps in the process. Between the steps, team members capture any physical travel that occurs, both of information and of people, as well as waiting and rework. On the steps and between the steps, the team members can mark downtime durations. They may note this from direct observation from the walk-through, or they may take it from the data collected during the preparation phase of the workshop.

Beneath each step, the team should place screen captures and/or hard-copy documents used in that particular step, when applicable. They should capture and print out every single screen that is accessed, used, or passed through.

Once the screen captures and forms are on the wall, the team tracks how information passes along the system, from screen to screen, from document to document. The team members do this with yarn or drawn lines. In this way, the team can see precisely how each data element flows (or doesn't flow–a "data dead-end"–see Chapter 2) through the process.

The *process-solution lane* is used as a "parking-lot" for possible solutions and for actual solutions that emerge from the following steps.

GO ON A PROCESS WALK

In a process walk, the team members walk through the process circumscribed by the charter, in the area where the work actually takes place. Run the scenario you have chosen through your system. As you run it through your system, capture copies of every single scrap of paper associated with completing the process. This may include forms, notes, yellow sticky-notes, cheat sheets, wall charts, reader boards, and so on. Print screen captures or readable digital photographs of every screen, menu, etc., are also used in the process. (You can capture reader boards, wall charts, and other large items with a print-out of a digital photograph of the item. Make sure that the data on the photograph can be read.)

This process walk gives the team an opportunity to see the whole process, preferably in action, together. The team members explain their part of the process to their teammates as they progress through the process. This helps team members learn about the process, as a whole, as opposed to only knowing their parts in the big picture.

This is also an opportunity for the team to learn from each other, become familiar with each other's role in the process, as well as get to know one another. Other benefits include being able to see the context in which the process actually occurs. Experiencing that in person has far more impact than just hearing about it. Also, people who are new to parts of the process will see that process with fresh eyes, lending their new perspective to the team. They may notice details that were missed in the initial data-gathering work. These details may help them develop better solutions.

The process walk helps people understand the process as a systemic phenomenon. The process happens by itself, but it also interacts with processes, systems, and people outside of itself. For some, *it may be the first time they see how what they do affects others* either upstream or downstream from themselves.

During the process walk, it is vital that the team takes notes about the process: the steps, ideas, waste, and so on. This information will be used in the next step, building a workflow chart.

ADD DATA TO THE PROCESS FLOW

Once the team members have seen the whole process, they are ready to add data to the process flow visualization. The data come from these sources:

- Information gleaned during the preparation phase

- Information and observations made during the process walk

The information from the preparation phase that you want to put on the visualization includes all of the following:

- People-flow information captured on the standard-operations combination sheet, including walking, working, and waiting

- Work-in-process

- The number of people required for each operation

- The metrics that are collected on the process

- Cycle times

Team members can add relevant information that they noticed on the process walk. The question to ask is, *"Does this information help me identify waste or other process issues?"*

When the team members have completed verifying the screen captures and populated the process visualization chart with the data, they are ready to identify waste and other process issues.

ANALYZE THE WORKFLOW

Once all the information is "on the wall," the team is ready to analyze the workflow. Here's a simple, straightforward way to do this:

- Ask the team to identify waste on the chart using sticky notes.

- Use your list of wastes to identify areas to improve.

- Keep the list of wastes available and visible for the team to use as they scan the process on the wall.

- Ask the team to place sticky notes in the area of the waste, with the specific waste marked on the sticky note. The chart should have a lot of sticky notes because every office process has lots of waste.

Then ask the five whys (5Ws). The five whys is a simple root-cause analysis technique where you ask the question "why" a number of times—five, as a rule of thumb—before arriving at the root cause of a problem. This curbs the tendency to jump to a conclusion based on preliminary observations. In a typical 5W exercise, the team members write down any specific problem that they come across. For example, they find an instance of waste. Then they ask why the problem occurs, and note the answer. Usually this does not lead the team to the root cause, so they consider the answer as another problem and ask "why?" This continues until the team is unanimously convinced that they have hit the root cause.

Here's a real example from an office environment:

Issue: Reports are inaccurate.

1. Why? Because the data is wrong.

2. Why is the data wrong? Because the data definitions in the data warehouse are unclear.

3. Why are they unclear? Because each department creates its own definitions without considering a standard.

4. Why do they create their own definitions without a standard? Because there are no standards.

5. Why are there no standards? Because no one can agree on what the standards should be.

6. Why can't they agree? Because the contributors to the data warehouse work for different departments with conflicting requirements and agendas.

This example could be taken further. However, it does show how even a complicated, systemic root cause can be identified through the simple five-why process.

GENERATE POSSIBLE SOLUTIONS

Generate possible solutions to resolve the waste issues. Any brainstorming technique can be used in this step.

There is a special tool to help nontechnical staff members participate in generating technical solutions. This tool, the system idea generator, is simply a list of questions to prompt thinking. See Figure 6–3 for sample questions.

As you can see from the list of questions in the figure, the workers' process knowledge is being leveraged against possible technical solutions. Even if most (or all) of the team members are not programmers or computing experts, they will usually have significant input for the solutions that will be generated.

1.   Is the process able to meet the business requirement?

2.   Is mistake-proofing built into the process?

3.   Does the process create a competitive or technological advantage?

4.   Do we understand the technology?

5.   Is the technology proven and reliable?

6.   Is the technology "low maintenance?"

7.   Is there a positive ROI?

8.   Is this a low-cost option?

9.   Does it simplify the process?

10.   Does it reduce the number of steps?

11.   Does is require a low level of approval to move forward?

12.   Is it better than a manual system in terms of quality, cost, and cycle time?

13.   Does it support one-piece flow?

14.   Does it support a pull system?

15.   Does it reduce or eliminate wastes in the categories of:

- Physical environment?

- Information processes?

- Business processes?

- People processes?

16.   Does it support the business strategy?

17.   Is it in alignment with our business values and ethics?

Figure 6-3. System Idea Generator

The intention is to have the solutions based on the actual requirements of the process and those that work within the process.

SIMULATE THE SOLUTIONS ("TRY-STORMING")

This next step is an important one. Simulating possible solutions is a powerful feature of lean. Simulation, in this case, means a rapid testing of the idea. Without spending too much time, do quick simulations of your identified solutions:

- Really walk through them.

- Time them.

- Gather the data using the same tool that you used when you collected data in the preparation phase.

This allows you to prove the concept before launch, increasing the likelihood of success when you do launch it.

Like the similarly named concept of brainstorming, *try-storming* refers to generating solutions and simulating them. The use of the term try-storming, rather than brainstorming, reflects a bias for *action*. Typically (although there are variations), in brainstorming, a team generates ideas—usually in a conference room, and somewhat independent of the right kind of data. In contrast, lean goes further and *tests out* the ideas. Untried ideas have little intrinsic practical value. They gain value as they are simulated—in other words, when they are tested for actual viability.

Unlike piloting a solution, simulation is a makeshift test produced hastily to get a sense of the viability of the solution before spending a lot of time and money running a pilot, which is more involved. There is nothing wrong with piloting, and that may be a feature of your implementation plan, but it is not to be done during the workshop.

When simulating in an office environment, you have to be creative. Use what you have and walk through the process improvement. For example, if you want to simulate a new paper form, modify an existing one by hand, or use a blank sheet of paper and a pencil. If you want to simulate a computer screen, use a sheet of paper, pencil, and, if you want, yellow sticky-notes.

When the solutions involve changes to a computing system, it is important to simulate those changes as well, step by step. The challenge here is to not *overproduce* the simulation by doing the simulation using computing equipment or software. It is sufficient to use modified screen captures from the existing systems, or to even create screens using paper and pencil.

Although the simulation is a hasty test, the team should collect process data to compare with the existing data on the process currently in place. This gives a basis for comparing solutions and their possible impact on the process.

The daily progress reports are based upon these simulations. This points to the importance of the simulations and the data collected during them. While the data from the simulations represent an *approximation* of what the actual implementation will be, these will be used as a benchmark and basis for determining the success of the implementation.

Build simulation screens using blank sheets of paper that one might use in a copier or printer. Oriented in landscape, the paper has the approximate dimensions (or at least aspect ratio) of the typical computer screen. The team can then use pencil and sticky notes to create a screen design. If a design does not work in the simulation, it can easily be modified with an eraser or a new sheet of paper.

PRIORITIZE YOUR SOLUTIONS

Most of the time, it is too unwieldy to address all of the wastes and solutions at the same time. Also, some solutions may prove difficult to implement, yet do not yield benefits commensurate to the effort.

A simple prioritization scheme may help teams prioritize the issues and solutions. The process consists of allocating all the issues/solutions sets they have in hand to one of four quadrants in a basic 2-5-2 matrix:

- High impact/low difficulty

- Low impact/low difficulty

- High impact/high difficulty

- Low impact/high difficulty

The team focuses on the first category, high impact/low difficulty, because these are the most feasible to do. Generally, the team will dismiss items that land in the low impact/high difficulty category as not worth the effort. They may then select some combination of the activities that have landed in the remaining two categories (see Figure 6-4).

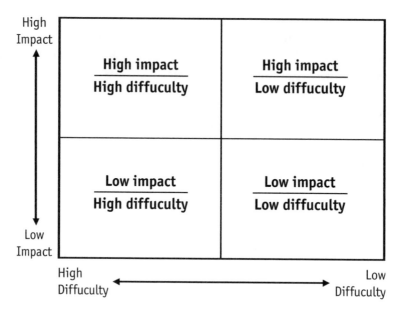

Figure 6-4. Impact/difficulty matrix

SELECT AND IMPLEMENT THE SOLUTIONS

The tradition of the kaizen is to implement the solutions immediately. This is possible because all the key stakeholders have been included in the preparation and workshop progress. The advantage of implementing a solution immediately is that it leverages the momentum gained during the workshop.

Once you have prioritized your solutions, select solutions the team can implement immediately, and then have the team implement them. For those solutions that cannot be implemented immediately, create an implementation schedule that includes the person responsible and the resources required to implement successfully.

Some solutions cannot be implemented immediately. In this case, implement everything that can be implemented and immediately start whatever is necessary to complete the total implementation. *This is critical.*

When the team has determined that some activities need to be done outside of the office kaizen workshop, it is the sponsor's responsibility to hold the team accountable for completion. Without the support of the sponsor in tracking progress of the implementation, the team may have trouble completing and maintaining the implementation. Implementation is a shared responsibility among all in the organization.

REPORT ON YOUR PROGRESS

Report-outs are informal, oral reviews of team progress. They are not written reports. Report-outs serve two functions:

- They provide a venue to regroup and review team progress.

- They provide a means of communicating to stakeholders.

Team members and subgroups need to communicate with one another at least daily. This ensures that the team members are learning from one another and are staying in step with one another's progress.

Report-outs also provide the means for the larger organization to keep informed of the team's progress, and to offer feedback for the team to consider. This will help the team develop solutions more readily accepted by the larger organization.

Daily Report-outs

If the kaizen lasts 3 days or more, conduct daily report-outs. The daily report-out is an informal report that shows the team's progress and the current state of affairs. This includes ideas being explored and simulated, and any obstacles that need attention or assistance.

The daily report-out also provides an opportunity for stakeholders, including the sponsor, other managers, and coworkers, to keep track of what is going on and to provide input and feedback.

Final Report-out

The final report-out is intended to bring all the work together into a cohesive, comprehensible whole. Knowing that they have to make a presentation to the sponsor on the work of the team serves as a great focusing and organizing force for the team.

A disciplined, well-organized report-out answers the key questions that the stakeholders, including the sponsor, may have about the proposed improvements and their implementation.

The report-out also generates confidence in the team and its product–the process improvements that the team members are implementing. This confidence engages others who are necessary for the successful implementation of the improvements.

An effective final report-out should include the following information:

- How the team functioned

- What challenges the team had to face

- How those challenges were overcome

- What challenges remain

- What plans are in place to address those challenges

This story is not an explicit part of the final report-out agenda. Rather, it is woven into the presented data. Accomplishments presented, along with the human experience that accompanied them, help people understand the reasoning for the team's conclusions, making acceptance easier for those not part of the workshop. It also helps the audience understand and appreciate how hard the team had to work to achieve their amazing results.

Figure 6-5 is a standard outline for a report-out, and the sections that follow explain why each item on this list is important.

---

1. Introductions
2. Charter
3. Team list
4. Daily progress report
5. Before data
6. After data
7. Improvements
8. Implementation plan
9. Action item list
10. Questions and answers
11. Team leader comments
12. Sponsor comments

Figure 6-5. Sample outline of a final report-out presentation

Describe the Charter of the Team and Introduce the Team Members
Go through the introductions, charter, and team list quickly as a review. The real meat of the report-out begins with the daily progress report. This is where the group can begin telling the story of what happened during the workshop and the final results.

Present the Before and After Data the Team Collected

Presenting the "before" and "after" data helps you explain how you achieved your results. When presenting the data, make sure that you make parallel comparisons. For example, if you decreased the amount of people walking by 60 yards, but your "before" data were measured in feet, then report your improvement in feet. In the case of this example, that would be 180 feet rather than 60 yards.

Describe the Improvements the Team Made

Now that you've shared your results, your audience will want to know how you got there. At this point in the report-out, share the specifics of your improvements. In sharing the improvements, people will want to know:

- What are the steps of the improvement

- How it impacts them

- What they have to do about it

- If any training is required—and if so, details

Describe Your Plan for Implementing Improvements

The next part of the report is the implementation plan. Much of what your team devises should be implementable immediately or shortly after the completion of the workshop. Remember—all who have been part of the solution have been part of the workshop in some way. The sponsor, who has authority over the process being improved, has sanctioned this event, approved the charter, and been following the progress of the workshop, providing perspective and assistance. Stakeholders have been kept abreast of progress, and those who actually work the process are part of the team. The colleagues of those on the team have also been tracking the progress of the team. All concerned need to know when to expect the action and the results.

Review the Action Item List

If something needs to be implemented later, track it on the action item list. Show the highlights of the action item list, explaining who will take responsibility for the items, and when the action will be implemented.

Open Up the Discussion to Q&A

Next is the question-and-answer period. Like the kickoff meeting, ground rules need to be established so that questions are reserved for the end, so that the team has an opportunity to share their material in its entirety. Capture questions asked during the report-out on a flip chart so that the meeting flow continues to move and then honor the question with an answer at the end.

Invite Comments from the Team Leader and Sponsor
By this time, you usually don't need to do any coaching; both the team leader and the sponsor are usually excited about the workshop and the results.

CONCLUSION

The next challenge for the organization is sustaining that excitement. In the heat of the workshop, energy is easy to ramp up. The challenge is to sustain commitment during the days and weeks after the workshop. Therefore, Chapter 7 deals with how to sustain lean improvements and a continuous improvement culture.

CHAPTER 7

SUSTAINING OFFICE KAIZEN IMPROVEMENTS

Contrary to popular opinion, the real work starts after the kaizen workshop is over. Because kaizen stands for *continuous incremental improvement*, sustaining the changes on a *continuous* basis is at the heart of the kaizen philosophy. Sustaining and building on office kaizen improvements, like any other kind of change, needs a support system. An effective system begins with a daily kaizen checklist (see Figure 7-1).[1] This checklist helps the implementing manager stay on track when implementing and sustaining the changes. This chapter describes the elements of such a checklist.

First week after kaizen
☐ Begin regular (weekly or biweekly) daily management meetings.
☐ Establish and document post-kaizen communication plan.
☐ Establish and document post-kaizen measurement plan.
☐ Schedule 6-month and 1-year report-out with executive team.
☐ Ensure proper documentation of new process.
☐ Establish method to collect input from process experts.
Second week after kaizen
☐ Survey process experts regarding implementation obstacles.
One month after kaizen
☐ Conduct one-month team review with sponsor to ensure implementation.
☐ Develop and deliver training in new methods.
☐ Continue regular (weekly or biweekly) daily management meetings.
Two months after kaizen
☐ Conduct 2-month team review with sponsor to ensure implementation.
☐ Continue regular (weekly or biweekly) daily management meetings.
Three months after kaizen
☐ Conduct 3-month team review with sponsor to ensure implementation.
☐ Continue regular (weekly or biweekly) daily management meetings.

Figure 7-1. Daily checklist for implementing and sustaining kaizen improvements

SCHEDULE "1-2-3 REPORTS"

Report-outs at 1-, 2-, and 3-month intervals provide an effective way to track and support sustained implementation of kaizen improvements. The sponsor and the team attend these "1-2-3 reports." The team reviews the original improvements, reports on progress, and identifies obstacles. The sponsor helps the team by removing obstacles and providing support, as appropriate. Together, they also analyze the kaizen event in itself, considering the following points:

- To what extent the kaizen met their expectations

- Which problem areas were not addressed

- What new issues, if any, came to light during the event

These report-out discussions often trigger the process of continuous change by highlighting new areas for improvement.

CONDUCT REGULAR STAND-UP MEETINGS FOR THE KAIZEN TEAM

Set regular stand-up meetings with the kaizen team. This can be done daily, weekly, or some interval in between. Although the frequency may differ, it is important to *schedule these meetings in advance* and *at regular intervals.*

Scheduling frequent, formal meetings may sound like a return to bureaucracy, but these meetings serve an important purpose. They help reiterate the action items and call for action to iron out minor glitches, before they balloon into major ones. They also ensure that the team stays involved and committed to the task undertaken.

At these stand-up meetings, teams should:

- Quickly go over progress against the action item list and obstacles

- Agree on a plan to address the obstacles

- Take appropriate action

- Then evaluate the consequence of this action

DOCUMENT THE NEW STANDARD PROCESS

Making changes in the process, and assessing their effectiveness is only one part of sustaining the kaizen effort. To complete the cycle, the new process should be *documented*. It is important to ensure that the documentation is as simple and clear as possible. Make the documented processes available and visible to all those affected by the process changes. Kaizen documentation should ideally follow the standard work format, clearly indicating the new standards for all of the following:

- Takt time

- Work-in-process

- The sequence of activities for performing a particular job

- Other variables, as applicable

True to the spirit of the "visual workplace," you can display the documented standards in appropriate locations so that any employee can refer to them at any time.

At all times, it is important to highlight that *these new standards are not etched in stone*. On the contrary, they provide the basis for *continuous improvement*.

STANDARDIZE AND IMPLEMENT A STATUS REPORTING SYSTEM

Create a simple way for management to keep track of progress on kaizen events. It is important to keep this simple for two reasons:

1. So that it is easy to grasp and deliver the message with no frills

2. So that it does not become a time-consuming task in itself. This would prove counterproductive, causing more waste, when the attempt, at all times, is to reduce waste.

A "stoplight chart," with color-coded red, yellow, and green indicators is sufficient. See Figure 7-2 for an example. Here are some other suggestions:

- Measure and quantify progress wherever possible.

- Set metrics for deliverables, like lead time and productivit, in the standard document, and measure them periodically.

- Address gaps, if any, and discuss solutions.

Project number	Project/ kaizen name	On track	Percent complete	Person responsible
1	Reduce order entry cycle time	● (green)	◗	Padma
2	5S mailroom	○ (red)	○	not yet assigned
3	Simplify engineering handoffs to sales	● (yellow)	◕	John
4	Delegate and train stock purchasing	● (green)	●	Karen

Figure 7-2. Sample lean implementation stoplight chart

IMPLEMENT COMMUNICATION AND TRAINING TO SUPPORT CHANGES

Communication is probably the most essential factor for sustaining any change. It is important that the right people know about the changes, how the changes impact them, and what they need to do differently. Again, the magic word is *"standardize."* The changes and their impact should be quantified and standardized, wherever possible, so that the benefits of *sustaining* the changes become evident. This ensures employee buy-in.

If people need to do something differently, here are some guidelines to ensure that the changes are implemented effectively:

- Make sure they know how to perform the new process or procedure.

- Clarify the specific roles of each employee in implementing and sustaining the changes.

- Provide employees with training, as and when required, to implement the new process.

A wrong but common assumption in this connection is that kaizen communication is a top-down affair. Although the sponsors or management play a significant role in clarifying goals and strategy, they are responsible for ensuring that the changes are clearly and uniformly communicated, and that the opinions and concerns of the employees are heard. All functional and hierarchical barriers to the flow of information and ideas should be removed. The employees should also be *actively involved* in identifying training needs and suggesting areas and methodology for learning and development. Remember that continuous improvement requires continuous communication. *Keep the communications channels open and accessible at all times.*

GET FEEDBACK—AND ACT ON IT!

It is impossible for any team to predict all the unintended consequences of changing a work system. That is why it is important to get feedback on the changes from those affected by the change, *especially from people who were not on the team*. The most common fallout is resistance, but some genuine, unanticipated obstacles may also arise when implementing the change.

Resistance to the new changes is to be expected, but do not dismiss it. Sometimes resistance is warranted. Investigate the issues that arise and deal with them accordingly. When a problem does crop up, all employees concerned should take part in devising solutions.

Kaizen is a cyclical and ongoing process. Thus, implementing a solution does not close the chapter forever. To ensure sustainable change, the team should make a habit of looking for potential loopholes and creating proactive solutions.

INTEGRATE KAIZEN IMPROVEMENTS INTO YOUR STRATEGIC FRAMEWORK

A basic assumption of all organizational change management theories is that no change can be sustained in isolation. In many organizations, when various strategic initiatives are implemented simultaneously, they end up vying with each other for resources and management buy-in. All conscious change efforts, including kaizen, should be viewed from the long-term strategic perspective, and they should together contribute to holistic organizational gains.

THE IMPACT OF SUSTAINING OFFICE KAIZEN IMPROVEMENTS

What is the impact of sustaining office kaizen improvements? You get better. It is that simple. The final and crucial step in the improvement process is choosing to sustain the change. This is not always easy, and will take learning and patience, but it is well worth the effort.

Although the objective of a kaizen event is to improve processes, physical aspects, and operational elements of work, it requires a c*hange in behavior and attitudes* to ensure that the improvements are sustained. Commitment to any change should emanate from the organization and the individual. This is true for kaizen and lean management techniques as well.

At the organizational level, top managers should see and understand the strategic relevance of a kaizen intervention, and they should provide sustained support and resources for the implementation of changes. They are responsible for communicating the proposed improvements and the expected benefits, in letter and spirit, across the organization.

The employees, for their part, should *own* the kaizen process, as well as the changes, and be committed to sustaining them. Resistance to change, to some extent, is woven into the human psyche. People may resist change because of fear, uncertainty, skepticism, and insecurity, among other reasons. However, when people realize that they have a significant role to play in making the change happen, and that ultimately, they stand to gain, they begin to accept the change. Once kaizen and lean gain this kind of emotional and cultural acceptance, you have progressed along the tracks of sustainable change. You will also rest easy in the knowledge that you have created a lean culture in your organization.

THE IMPORTANCE OF *PEOPLE* IN SUSTAINING LEAN

The beginning of this book emphasized the relative ease of process improvement once a person knows the principles of lean. The hard part is people.

Without people buy-in, lean is diluted. And interestingly, without lean, people's joy in their work is diluted. Lean creates a space where people blossom, and where they can fully express their talents and capacities.

Any lean effort is sustainable only when employees become comfortable around the lean process and resulting change. Comfort levels cannot be achieved unless lean is practiced widely and over a length of time. The good news is that this is not altogether impossible.

THE IMPACT OF THE CHANGE ON PEOPLE

Understanding that changes in the work processes impact the people who will perform those processes is critical to the success and sustainability of lean. Adopting a parallel human dynamics management tool as you implement lean would be highly beneficial—like a primer that prepares people for the changes ahead. With a good change management tool, you can accomplish all of the following:

- Avoid at least some, if not all, problems, challenges, and conflicts associated with lean implementation.

- Ensure that everyone is involved, if not sold, on the wave of new ideas and is therefore able to better implement the same.

- Provide general and specific clarity around the role everyone will play in achieving the success that the lean implementation promises the firm.

This will ensure that you are ready to create the lean culture at your organization—a culture where lean and kaizen are ongoing, and employees own the initiatives as much as—if not more than—the senior management.

FROM THE AUTHOR

I hope you have found this book supportive and encouraging. There is a lot to learn about lean, but the benefits are exciting and well worth it. I wish you the best on your lean journey!

— Carlos Venegas (www.strausforest.com)

NOTES

1. Ann (Callaghan) Dorgan, "Improving Rapid Process Improvement Sustainability Processes within a Hospital Setting" (Master's thesis, Leadership Institute of Seattle, 2005).

APPENDIX: TEAM TIPS

You've done all the groundwork, you've contacted all the right people, you have the right people on the team, and you have sponsorship for your lean initiative. You've thought of everything, right? Not quite.

Inevitably, you have not thought of everything, because every lean workshop poses different circumstances. However, any circumstance will not be an obstacle to your event if you and your team understand *the need to be flexible and responsive to any issue that may arise*. Some important factors that may contribute to the success of your event include:

- A "just-do-it" spirit

- A team dinner

- A team kickoff

- Just-in-time training

ENCOURAGE A "JUST-DO-IT" SPIRIT

One of the most powerful dynamics involved in with kaizens of any kind, whether in the office or factory, is the "just-do-it" mentality. No one needs to wait for obstacles to be removed by someone else or for an approval to try something out. In the try-storming process (see **Simulate the Solutions** ["Try-storming"] in Chapter 6), the team can experiment with a number of options quickly. For example, one team evaluated two solutions to one part of an order-entry process—one was manual, the other partially automated. They were advised by the author of this book to try both of them, gathering data as they did it, so they would have some basis of comparison.

In the situation just described, the team members started out debating the merits of the two options. One required manual checking, the other required a few more steps. Facilitators need to be aware that at times, the team may want to process or discuss whether or not to try an idea. Teams will sometimes spend much more time *discussing* whether or not to try an idea than it would take to *simulate* the idea! I suppose it is a learned habit—to not do things unless you are sure that they work. However, you need to fight this tendency, and encourage the team to "just do it" and take action. After the team discussed the pros and cons of each for a short while (until they started repeating their ideas), they were encouraged to try-storm and collect data.

People may also reactively shy away from the mistakes of the pilot for fear of punishment or rejection. In some companies employees learning lean implementation were tentative when it came to making decisions or acting without management approval. One group, experimented with the height of a worktable used for processing paperwork associated with checking in video rentals being returned to the warehouse. The tables were too low for some, causing some workers back strain as they bent over to work. When it was suggested that they simulate working with adjustable tables, they said that management would never invest in adjustable tables. Their concern, driven by budget realities, was justified. However, I reminded them that the experimental process of "try-storming" is risk free. In a simulation, you do not actually *change* the process—you simply *simulate* the planned change in the process, and collect data on the results of the change. This gives management hard data on productivity and safety against which they can weigh other business priorities.

At times, a team member may whole-heartedly believe that the idea won't work. Don't let this stop you from doing the simulation. For example, David, a production scheduler, who thought that he was doing things the best possible way, had been in the industry for more than 25 years, and was among the most knowledgeable. He whole-heartedly believed that lean had nothing to offer him or his process. It took a while, but after learning more about lean, and after collecting data on a few simulations, he came to value the improvements that were possible by applying lean principles.

Even if the person ends up being right about a particular idea not being viable, the simulation may generate an idea that is even better than the first one. I would venture to say that *the more you simulate, the more you learn.* And the more you learn, the better your final results. It stands to reason that improvement is a learning process. Focus on learning a lot about what does not work as well as what does. You won't lose any "points" for a simulation that doesn't yield the results for which you had hoped.

HOLD A TEAM DINNER

During a 4- or 5-day kaizen workshop, try to go to dinner as a team on the evening of the second day of the workshop. There is an interesting dynamic associated with both the second day of the workshop and the evening dinner.

The second day of the workshop seems to mark the "storming" phase of the team's development. The team is faced with goals that may seem unreachable; they may be using tools that are new to them; or it may simply be a phase that most teams go through. In any event, is the second day of the workshop seems to be the crazy day.

The evening dinner on the second day of the workshop gives people a chance to unwind together. As cliché as this may sound, it is a bonding time. People talk about the day; they also talk about personal things. I think there is a humanizing process that happens when people share a meal together away from the workplace.

Come day three of workshop, the team coalesces around the project. People seem to get along better and become more productive. There is nothing scientific about this suggestion.

SCHEDULE A TEAM KICKOFF

The team kickoff is an important part of the workshop. It helps the team form around the objectives of the charter. It also serves as an important opportunity for the sponsor of the project to demonstrate his or her support, to put the project in the larger organizational context, and to verbally sanction the formation and goals of the team. One sponsor, Jack, did this particularly well. He was the director of a business unit within a Fortune 500 multinational. He attended every team kickoff and explained the importance of each team's business objective in the context of the business unit's strategy and goals. He also fielded questions from the team.

The kickoff should be no longer than 20 minutes. Usually the sponsor delivers a message, and the team leader presents the charter and a summary of the data collected during the preparation phase. The kickoff is also a time for everyone to ask questions of clarification.

DELIVER JUST-IN-TIME TRAINING

When delivering just-in-time training, try to make it as interactive as possible. In other words, give people an opportunity to apply what they are learning to real-world experiences. For example, when teaching about waste, send the team on a "waste walk" through a preapproved work area (as discussed in detail in chapter 6).

Give frequent breaks—about 5 to 10 minutes per hour. This may not be a normal break schedule; what matters is that it is effective in boosting the team's productivity. Adult learning theory tells us that frequent breaks in the learning process help increase knowledge acquisition and retention.

If you are having a longer workshop—say, 3- to 5-days—you can break up the training. Start the training with what people need to know to get started, and present new information over the course of the workshop, as they need it. For example, don't train team members on simulation techniques until they are ready to actually do simulations.[1]

My encouragement to you is to approach lean as an exciting learning opportunity. Develop your own team tips based on your own experience. I'm interested in your learning and your experiences. Share what you've learned by emailing me at carlos@strausforest.com.

NOTES

1. I didn't always do it this way. I recall that on my first lean implementation, I put 75 production workers and managers through 8 hours of training. For some in the class, it would be months before they would use the material, and months since they had forgotten the material. Since then, I've learned to apply just-in-time lean thinking to the training process.

GLOSSARY

LEAN MANAGEMENT TERMS

Continuous Flow: Uninterrupted movement of any product, service, or element through the value stream—also known as one-piece flow.

Five Ss: A tool for elimination of waste; an abbreviation that stands for *sort, simplify, sweep, standardize,* and *sustain.*

Five Whys: The technique of asking, "Why?" at least five times to find the root cause of a problem.

Just-in-Time (JIT): A technique that makes resources available only as and when they are required. Applied to products and services, it implies producing or delivering just the required quantity at the right time.

Pacemaker: The point in the value stream that is scheduled, in order to regulate the flow of work.

Pitch: The pace and flow of a product or service grouping.

Process Walk: The act of physically going through and observing a process to understand it better.

Standard Work: Documented form of best practices, usually including standards for takt time (see the following glossary of non-English terms for a definition), the steps in a process, and the amount of work that should be in the system at any point of time.

Toyota Production System (TPS): The production system pioneered by Taiichi Ohno at the Toyota Motor Company.

Try-storming: Simulation of a solution.

Value Stream: The set of all activities that constitute a business process.

Visual Controls: Visual feedback devices that indicate the current status of work.

Work Cell: A group of equipment or people who perform similar tasks or are responsible for a common outcome.

NON-ENGLISH WORDS AND PHRASES

Heijunka (hey-june-kah): Japanese term for workload leveling—the process of smoothing out production to ensure a uniform flow of work over time.

Jidoka (ji-doh-kah): Autonomation, or automation with a human touch.

Kaizen (ky-zen): An approach to productivity that aims for continuous, incremental improvement.

Kanban (kahn-bahn): A visual signal that indicates the demand for an item—also known as the "pull" system.

Muda (moo-da): Japanese term for waste—anything that does not add value or blocks the flow of value.

Poka Yoke (poh-kah yoh-kay): Mistake proofing—preventing mistakes by designing the process in a way that it becomes impossible to continue the process if a mistake has been made.

Takt (tact) Time: The rate of customer demand. Takt time is calculated this way:

Takt time = productive time available per day/customer demand per day

INDEX

ABOUT THE AUTHOR

Carlos Venegas, president of Straus/Forest, LLC, has helped scores of clients implement successful process-improvement initiatives in a wide range of organizations: from 1,000-employee business units in a Fortune 500 company to a four-employee firm. The range of businesses with which Carlos has worked includes technical and engineering design, creative services, building and maintenance contractors, interior design, retail, aerospace manufacturing, inventory management, printers, electronics assembly, accounting and finance, human resources, and IT, to name a few.

In addition to nonfactory kaizens, consultations have included strategy alignment, tactical planning, employee involvement and engagement, communication, and shop-floor kaizen. As a lean leadership coach, Carlos has helped many individuals achieve their organizational goals. His clients include top executives in a Fortune 500 company, executives in large and small nonprofits, entrepreneurs, small-business owners, and private individuals.

Carlos has an M.A. in applied behavioral science. He has also received extensive lean training from Shingijutsu, Ltd., both in Japan and the United States.

Carlos may be contacted by e-mail at carlos@strausforest.com or through the Straus Forest Web site: www.strausforest.com